DESERT TREKS
from Jeddah

PATRICIA BARBOR

Contents

TRAVEL DOCUMENTS

Antiquity Sites

To visit Medain Saleh, al Ula (page 20), the old Hejaz Railway station (page 26) and Qalat Tabuk a letter of permission is required.

A formal letter should be written on behalf of the leader of the party by his Saudi sponsor,and should be addressed to the Assistant Deputy Minister for Antiquities and Museum Affairs in Riyadh (address below).

The letter must be submitted at least 15 days before the proposed visit.

The names of all the visitors, their nationalities, passport numbers and the plate numbers of their vehicles should be mentioned in the letter.

The proposed date of visit and duration of stay is also required.

The letter can be delivered by hand to the museum in Shamaisy Street or by mail or fax:

Address: P.O. Box 3734   Fax: 01 411 2051
               Riyadh 11481

The Telephone number of the Department is: 01 411 5777, ext. 233

Foreigners are advised to carry with them a travel letter signed and stamped by their sponsor if they are driving further than 50 km from Jeddah.

SAFETY

Safety Hints When you travel off the roads, always go with at least one other vehicle.

- Sleep off the ground if possible. If not, sleep inside a tent sealed against scorpions and snakes.
- Take special care where you sit, place your hands, etc.
- Use a flashlight/torch for night walking.
- When accompanied by children, be constantly vigilant of them.
- Take plenty of water and, in summer, head covering.
- Tell someone where you are going.
- If you break down, never walk away from your vehicle to seek help: it is too easy to get lost and dehydration occurs very rapidly in summer.
- Never take your shoes off in sand dunes as the horned viper can lurk just beneath the surface: always wear high-topped, protective lace-up shoes.
- Bilharzia (transmitted via snails) occurs in still water in various parts of Arabia. Those wading or bathing may wish to be checked for the disease in the case of any symptoms appearing.

Warning: When camping, avoid wadi beds during the rainy season as there is a real danger of flash floods. Be careful when driving over sabkha (dried up salt-marsh) as the ground can be treacherously soft under the crust.

Vehicle Equipment We strongly recommend you take with you on your desert trek:

- Shade (awning or side cover)
- Compass
- Spade or shovel
- Spare tyre(s)
- Radiator leak sealant
- Sand ladders and tow rope
- Engine spares
- Oils and coolant
- Air compressor for re-inflating tyres

Camping Check List It is useful to make a checklist before leaving. It is easy to forget something. Here is one for comfortable camping, which you can adapt as you wish.

Kettle	Water for drinking	Torches
Saucepans	Water for washing	Candles
Frying pan	Food in cool boxes	Matches
Cooking utensils	Salt and pepper	Paper for fire
Plates	Coffee	Wood for fire
Cups	Tea	Mosquito nets and
Knives, forks	Milk	repellent
and spoons	Sugar	Tent, pegs, guy
Washing up liquid	Washing kit and towel	ropes
Washing up cloths	Sleeping bags	Camel rugs
Washing up bowl	Camp beds	Light with fuel
Tea towel	Table	Cameras, films
Tin opener	Loo paper	Furrwa or warm
Pillows	Compass and maps	clothing
Rubbish bag	Hats, sunglasses	First aid kit

Suggestions for first aid kit

Aspirin	Dettol and antiseptic cream	Scissors
Elastoplast	Sling	Needle and thread
Sterile bandages	Safety pin	Soap
Cotton wool	Eye drops	Snake bite kit
Tweezers	Matches	

Please respect the natural history of the Kingdom. Do not damage vegetation or kill wild animals. When visiting an archaeological site, do not remove artefacts and be very careful not to damage the remains.

It is forbidden to publish photographs of or articles about the sites without permission from the Ministry.

Take only memories: leave only footprints.

1 Moon Mountain, al Maqar

DAY TRIP (1 hr)

2 WHEEL DRIVE

In the hills above al Maqar, only 45 minutes from Jeddah, there is an area of white sandy ground and pale smooth rocks worn into bizarre shapes, a huge adventure playground for the imaginative child or quiet contemplative refuge for the work-weary adult. It is a moonscape of colourless boulders, some eroded to form little caves, some piled in outcrops to present challenges for young climbers. Towering above them all is a round-topped cone or pinnacle of bald rock, behind which one must drive to find this quiet refuge.

It is an excellent place to escape to from the confines of the city for a picnic during the day. There are a few low trees, but not a great deal of shade, so an awning may be advisable. It is also a marvellous place for an evening picnic and would be particularly atmospheric by moonlight. Being close to a road and only a short distance from Jeddah, it is perfectly possible for those who prefer their own beds to return to Jeddah the same night. For those who favour star-gazing from their pillows (watching for shooting stars can have as somnolent an effect as counting sheep and is far more rewarding), it is a good camping site.

We were told of this site by friends who take the boy scouts to camp here and indeed it has all the marks of a good scout camp. It is spotlessly clean, with the occasional neat ring of stones encircling the ashes and charcoal remains of wood fires. There is none of the litter of the thoughtless camper. If you want to light a fire, take some wood with you.

Moon Mountain

Take the road north from Jeddah to Usfan. SET YOUR ODOMETER AT **0** at the junction of the ring road expressway, the al Haramain road and the Usfan road.

At 5 km on the Usfan road is a police checkpoint.

At 27 km drive over the Makkah/Medina road and follow the road bearing to the left to Usfan.

Drive through Usfan and at about 34 km you will see a big blue square sign on the right of the road. It is in Arabic with a long white arrow pointing right and the bottom two lines read 'al Kamil, 82 km'. Take this turn to the right.

Follow the road rising into the hills for about 20 km and at 53.8 km you will see the smooth round-topped pinnacle of rock just off the road to the left. Leave the road when you are abreast of the pinnacle. It will now become hidden by an outcrop of rocks, where there is a track. This is important if you are in a 2-wheel drive. If you leave the road before this point, the sand is soft and you may sink in. Follow the track round behind the pinnacle, where you are well hidden from the road.

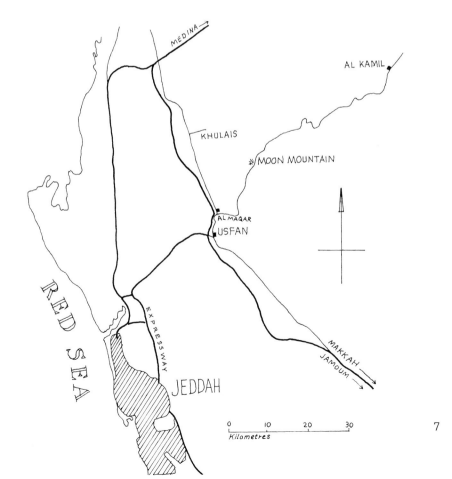

2 **Marble Mountain, Madrakah**

DAY OR WEEKEND TRIP (1½-2 hrs)

2 WHEEL DRIVE

Out of the lava fields 60 km north-north-east of Makkah, at about 3000 ft. above sea level, rises the marble mountain of two or three hundred feet. Much of the marble has been quarried and many huge square blocks of white marble, now apparently abandoned, lie like some ancient ruined city at the foot of the mountain. Camp there when the moon is full to capture the mystery and magic of the white mountain, as it glows in the moonlight.

You will have reached the place via the little town of Madrakah, from where the track rises onto a high plain of sand and scrub, and thence to the lava fields. The lava here appears not to have erupted and flowed down conical shaped volcanoes, as I, in my ignorance, presumed but issued from huge rifts in the ground, where it congealed and broke into dark brown and black boulders as it cooled. As you drive along the track in the evening, across the sandy plain, your first sight of the mountain is quite dramatic: a solitary white form caught in the rays of the setting sun, rising from a dark plateau.

You can camp to the left of it, on the edge of a ravine with a fine view westwards towards the mountains and the setting sun. Alternatively if you move round further to the north of the mountain, there are dips in the ground, where you would be more sheltered and possibly find shade from the morning sun.

Although referred to as "the mountain", it is in fact little more than a craggy mound. It is a short scramble to the top or an easy walk up a spiralling track made to bring the quarried marble down.

There are a surprising number of different types of flora growing amongst the marble boulders. Even on the flattened top are large clumps of *aloe rubrovio-laceae*. In April we heard the distinctive call and saw flights of bee-eaters. Little swifts were swooping low over the rocks and we heard a hoopoe calling.

Wood can be found for a fire amongst the abandoned and ruined houses of the quarrymen.

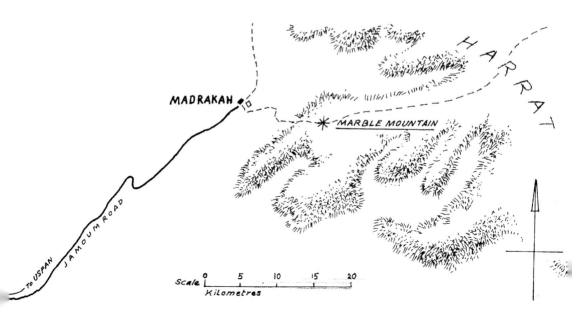

DIRECTIONS ▶

From Jeddah take the Medina road heading north. Turn right for Usfan beyond the northern end of Jeddah's Abdul Aziz Airport. At this junction with the ring road SET YOUR ODOMETER AT **0**.

Drive for 28 km heading for Usfan. Just before you get into Usfan, take a right turn signposted to Shamiyah.

After 31 km more, you will see a sign to Hada al Sham pointing left. Take this turn and immediately you will see another sign - straight on to "Hada A'Sham 16 kms" and "Madrakah 63 kms."

When you reach Madrakah, take a turn right towards the most prominent mosque, the tallest, whitest one in the centre of the town and, leaving it to your left, follow the track over the horizon.

Now you drive up and on for 13 km until you almost run into the white marble mountain at odometer reading 135 km.

Marble Mountain

3 Wadi Khulais

DAY TRIP (1½ hrs)

2 WHEEL DRIVE

This is an area of particular interest to bird watchers - a haven for migrating birds and a breeding ground for birds nesting in the trees, shrubs and sandbanks.

The land is fertile, fed by underground water and water running from the many narrow wadis to the east. Apparently this was once the source of water for the city of Jeddah. Sometimes water remains in large pools long after the rains have fallen. Here "instant fish", the shrimp-like *triops granarius,* and toads abound. The toads burrow deep into the wet sand to re-emerge after the dry periods. The "fish" have a fast life-cycle. Their tiny grain-sized eggs can lie dormant in dry sand or mud for up to 15 years; but when the rain falls, they must hatch, grow to maturity and lay their eggs before the water evaporates again. Water birds, such as herons, are attracted here by the rich source of food.

Wadi Khulais

Even when the pools are dry there are many beautiful birds to be seen: the exquisite little green bee-eaters, orange-tufted sunbirds, the superb hoopoes, black bush robins, shrikes, Ruppel's weavers, bulbuls and sand partridges.

Even after a prolonged dry period in Wadi Khulais, one may still find flowers, such as the bright yellow *acacia mimosa,* the beautiful pinks and reds of the *capparis decidua,* the delicately branched *heliotropium longiflorum* and the tough little blooms of the *fagonia indica.*

The campsites chosen here are on slightly raised ground, a precaution against flash floods, which can arrive without warning from rain falling many miles away. They are also chosen for their views, shade and access to good climbs up the rocky hills into the gorge of the second campsite.

Campsite 1 has an additional point of interest. On a rockface to the left as you look into the sandy wadi, about 15 ft. above the ground, is a small area covered by ancient carved graffiti. Two camels are clearly distinguishable amongst script which appears to run vertically.

There is a plenty of wood for campfires, but if tempted by the pools, remember bilharzia.

THUWAL

Scale
0   10   20
Kilometres

CAMPSITE I

Water Tower Fort   CAMPSITE II

KHULAIS

To JEDDAH   USFAN

Leave Jeddah heading north along the Medina road. Turn right onto the Usfan road beyond the northern end of Jeddah's King Abdul Aziz Airport. SET YOUR ODOMETER AT **0**.

At 38.5 km, approximately 10 km beyond Usfan, is a junction with the Medina/Makkah expressway and the sign straight on to Khulais. Continue another 17 km, passing through the first part of Khulais. Look out for the sign reading "SLOW DANGEROUS DESCENT 500 METRES". Continue 1.5 km beyond this sign and turn right.

Follow the road nearly 4 km into the small village and turn left at a crossroads opposite a mosque on the right. Drive for about 1 km, some of which is a short switchback, until the road forks at a round monument with Khulais written in Arabic. Fork right and almost immediately turn right again off the road onto a rough but well defined stony track, passing a 25 metre water tower on the left.

Continue for another 2 km and you will see the remains of an old Turkish fort, standing high on an outcrop of rock on the left.

You are now in a very wide wadi and the track is bordered by low trees. The wadi closes in a little after about 12.5 km and is bounded by high granite hills. Look to the left where you will see a break in the hills and a bank of sand at the junction of a side wadi, on which stand two palm trees together plus a cluster of another half a dozen to one side. About 0.5 km across the wadi from this point is Campsite 1. There is a short red striped concrete post and a capped well, a slab with K 83 painted on it, to the left of the track a few metres further on.

Turn off the track and cross the very rough and stony wadi, which is just possible for a 2-wheel drive vehicle if you choose your route with care. It would probably be unwise to attempt to drive up the bank of sand by the palm trees, unless in a 4-wheel drive.

To reach Campsite 2, return to and continue along the main track, passing a farm on the left, 2.5 km on, comprising what appear to be hen houses, a long concrete shed, a habitable building and one decidedly uninhabitable derelict building. Slightly more than 3.5 km from here, the wadi swings round to the left and on the left, where the track nudges against the cliff, is a lone palm tree. Just beyond it is another low concrete post marked with K93. Look to the right across rough and stony ground and the wet sand wadi bed about 0.5 km towards sandbanks, where a gorge in the hills and a narrow wadi open up into the wide one. Here on higher ground, by the shade of the acacias, is Campsite 2. Again, proceed with caution if you are in a 2-wheel drive. The one in our party successfully negotiated the wadi bed, but stuck once in a soft sandbank and had to be towed out!

4 Wadi Mur

WEEKEND TRIP (2-2½ hrs)

4 WHEEL DRIVE

This is a lovely campsite on the banks of the water running down from the harrat or lava fields, which stretch far away on either side.

Driving from the direction of Rabigh, the flat gravelly plain with gloomy stretches of black basalt rising ahead looks to the visitor very unpromising. However, as the track straddles the ridge, one is rewarded with a dramatic and encouraging view of a sandy plain, humped with small hills and a scattering of acacias. This plateau lies on the west bank of the wadi and stretches many kilometres to the south, flanked by the harrat.

In descending from the ridge and driving eagerly towards the palm trees, which indicate where the stream lies, it would not be difficult to drive over the edge of the sand cliff !

Coming from one direction you are on the edge of the plateau before you realise you are so close to the water, which was hidden from view in the gully.

You can camp anywhere along the bank. We chose a site on sandy rocks slightly above the river bed, facing a cluster of palm trees on the far bank with a backdrop of sandstone cliffs, tinged with red and gold. In the deeper pools were large clumps of reeds and bulrushes, which suggests there is water here for much of the year. In late March when we were there, we suspected it had rained in the hills a few days before, as the water was flowing swiftly over the stony shallows and gushing through narrow gullies and over mini rapids. The sound of rushing water, accompanied by the croak of toads and rattle of frogs at night, was a pleasant change from the usual stillness of a desert night. However, only a fortnight later the water had reduced dramatically and the quieter water produced troublesome mosquitoes, which were blown away by a cold wind later in the night.

It seemed the water had worn the sandy rocks into interesting shapes in some previous rainier periods. We were nearly fooled into thinking we had found the site of some building of antiquity, as we gazed at what we thought had to be man-made bases of ancient pillars, so perfectly circular and identical were they. As for the wildlife, we saw myriads of tiny toads, a few small frogs, little "instant fish" and water boatmen sculling through the water. There were some dragonflies, red and turquoise, and at night we glimpsed bats darting across the stars. We disturbed a number of egrets, flocks of Arabian babblers, swifts, shovelers, a great grey shrike, a harrier and one little green bee-eater.

Wadi Mur

Apart from the *acacia mimosa*, the only flowers seen were beautifully camouflaged tiny pink blooms in sandy grey leaves, lying flat on the sand, some bearing flowers and seedpods together.

Although on our first visit the water in the main stream was flowing fast and looked exceedingly enticing, especially as the sun rose higher, apparently there is still a danger of bilharzia, so it is advisable to resist the temptation to wallow and splash in the shallows.

DIRECTIONS

Drive north out of Jeddah on the Medina road. SET YOUR ODOMETER AT **0** at the junction of the ring road expressway, the al Haramain road and the Medina or al Munawwarah road. There is a police checkpoint just beyond it.

Continue north for 54 km. Turn left for Thuwal, Qadimah and Rabigh. At 56 km, turn right to Qadimah and Rabigh. Drive straight on under an army of electricity pylons marching four abreast across the desert from the Steam Power Plant at about 100 km. At 105 km, drive past the right turn to Johfah. At 115 km, as you approach a small town or suburb of Rabigh, there is a large blue sign written in Arabic with directions to the refinery, which you will see in the distance on your left. Turn right here. SET YOUR ODOMETER AT **0**.

At 16.3 km you will reach what is called "the Irish bridge". On our first trip there was no sign of a bridge; instead we had to ford a fast running river of water. Two weeks later when the water had subsided the bridge manifested itself. Cross through or over the water! After about 0.3 km turn right off the road onto a track heading east. RE-SET YOUR ODOMETER AT **0**.

Follow the track, heading predominantly S.S.E. After approximately 10 km you will see an oasis and palms to your right. This is the farming settlement of Haqqaq. Leaving Haqqaq on your right, the track leads up rising ground through the basalt boulders. Suddenly at 14.6 km on the crest of the hill, the view opens onto an entirely different landscape, a humpy sandy plateau, scattered with low acacias. Looking down and to the right, you will see a group of palm trees, sandstone cliffs and sand dunes beyond. Head for the palm trees and here in about 1.3 km you should find the waters of Wadi Mur.

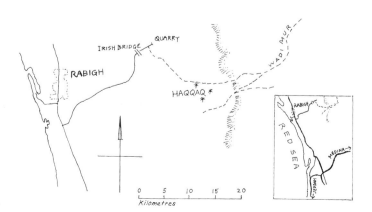

13

5 Wadi Uranah and al Shafa

DAY TRIP (1 hr)

2 WHEEL DRIVE

To get the best out of a day's bird watching, an early start is obviously advisable, if not essential. Leaving Jeddah at 5.30 or 6.00 am on a Friday is a joy with so little traffic on the road.

The first stop on this trip is on the non-Muslim Makkah by-pass heading towards Taif, about 3.5 km beyond where it leaves the Makkah road. Look carefully at a big boulder close to the rocky outcrop about 100 metres to the left and you are very likely to see a little owl perched on top. He is nearly always there at this time in the morning, surveying the world in his wise way.

Continue on the by-pass until you reach Wadi Uranah, in which lies the waste water flowing down from Makkah. It has formed a big lake with low reedy islands wonderfully rich in bird life. On our first trip we saw more than 24 different species within half an hour. Among the most notable were the squacco herons, pallid harriers, chestnut-bellied sand grouse and glossy ibis.

At the top of the escarpment, having driven up the terrifyingly steep hairpinned road, a climb of a few thousand feet, drive off to the left just before the fruit market, avoiding the voracious baboons, who are masters in the art of stealing fruit and jars of honey. They prefer the honey with nuts, which they will pick from the bottom of the pile! Then descend onto a rock platform where there was once a restaurant. Here you have a magnificent view and a chance to see more birds swooping and gliding below, such as pale crag martins, Tristram's grackles, hoopoes and fan-tailed ravens.

From here it is a short drive to al Shafa, which, with its good tarmac road from al Hada and Taif, has become a popular picnic place in the summer. By

Wadi al Uranah

lunchtime, families have spread out in the shade of the trees within easy distance of the road to enjoy the cool air of the mountains. In al Shafa itself there is plenty of entertainment for children including playgrounds and donkey and camel rides. Drive round on the looping road and turn off from al Shafa for a short distance and there is still an abundance of birds to be seen, particularly where there is water caught in the gorges and rock pools. Among many species seen on our visit were a Yemen linnet, an olive-rumped serin, a cinnamon-chested rock bunting and an Abyssinian white-eye or zosterops. This pretty little bird with its distinctive white eye-ring is a common resident in Asir.

We had with us a keen and experienced bird watching friend from England and at the end of the day, when about fifty different species had been identified, he was delighted that, of those, over twenty were first sightings for him.

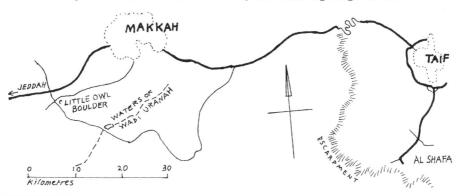

DIRECTIONS

Leave Jeddah on the Makkah expressway. SET YOUR ODOMETER AT 0 by the palm sculpture at the junction with al Falah Street.

At about 40 km turn right onto the non-Muslim by-pass and drive off the left side of the road after 3 km, just beyond the Gizan turning, where, at the foot of rocky outcrops you may see the little owl.

Continue on the same road. At 55 km you should reach Wadi Uranah on the left of the road. Drive on towards Taif and up the escarpment. At the top, on the very last bend, is the leftward turn to the platform with the ruined restaurant, but to get there you must drive on, turn off at the al Hada ring road at 145 km, cross the road and come back to the turn-off. Then drive down a rough road about 200 metres to park.

Return to the main road and turn right until you can do a U-turn before continuing on the road towards Taif. Approximately 16 km further on is the turn-off to the right to al Shafa. After 12.5 km turn right again for al Shafa.

The road through al Shafa goes round in a loop and when you have circled al Shafa your odometer reading will be about 193 km.

Take any of the turnings off the road to find a nice picnic site.

6 Khaybar, Village and Dam

WEEKEND TRIP (6½-7 hrs)

4 WHEEL DRIVE

"The large Kheybar valleys lie together, like a palm leaf, in the Harra border: they are gashes in the lava field....." So wrote Charles Doughty in "Travels in Arabia Deserta".

Khaybar, which was once a Jewish settlement, is a well-watered oasis and village cluster lying in the harrat, the black volcanic lava fields, north of Medina near the highway to Tabuk. Fed by many springs, it has been an agricultural area since pre-Islamic times. In c. 552 BC it was conquered by Nabonidus, the last king of the Neo-Babylonians. Some say it was from his army that the Jewish settlers came.

More recently, three well known European travellers visited and wrote of Khaybar. The first was Carlo Guarmani, an Italian, in search of pure Arabian horses, in 1864.

Then came Charles Doughty, the great English writer on Arabia, in 1877. From the beginning he disliked Khaybar intensely. His belongings, books and money were taken from him and he was held captive here for as long as three months, in fear for his life. He wrote at length of his time in Khaybar, with vivid descriptions of the inhabitants, their dwellings and way of life under the Dowla or Ottoman government.

Towards the end of 1950, St. John Philby spent four days in Khaybar, arriving at Christmas on a map-making expedition from Riyadh to Medina. Finding rock drawings, but no inscriptions at Khaybar, he wondered if the early inhabitants, the Jews, kept records on papyrus or palm fronds.

Having seen the pre-Islamic dams, which he thought might have been built to accumulate silt for upstream plantations, he concluded that in Jewish times agriculture must have been more widespread.

According to Doughty there were three villages, named after the *"land-inheriting Annezy tribes"*, Jeriat Bishr, Jeriat W. Aly and Jeriat el-Fejir.

Bishr, the main and largest village of 200 houses or more, lies in a depressed area of land and its many springs and occasional rain water can cause unpleasant swamps. So in recent times the Saudi government built a new town on higher ground, 5 km to the south, into which the inhabitants were moved, leaving Bishr abandoned and desolate. It does indeed have a haunted and eerie atmosphere. All sound is swallowed up in the narrow streets, so that once round a corner, still close to, but out of sight of, others, there seems a deathly silence.

At what point the Jews were finally driven out is uncertain. Doughty writes of the *"squalid ground, stained with filthy rust: whence their fable, that 'this earth purges herself of the much blood of the Yahud, that was spilt in the conquest of Kheybar'"*.

The Qasr Marhab, or Jews' castle, or citadel, stands high on what are thought to be pre-Islamic foundations, overlooking the houses and latter-day mosque. Marhab was the last shaikh of old Jewish Khaybar. Beside the mosque is the burial ground with many small piles of grave stones.

Some of the houses, still standing firmly, are worth inspection. They have small, dark rooms with stone stairways leading to the first upper floor only. *"The lower floor in these damp oases,"* wrote Doughty, *"is a place where they leave the orchard tools, and a stable for their few goats......Our host's upper room was open at the street side with long casements, taga, to the floor, his roof was but a loose strawing of palm stalks, and above is the house terrace of beaten clay, to which you ascend by a ladder of two or three palm beams with steps hacked in them."*

To Doughty, Khaybar appeared *"as it were an African village in the Hejaz "* of which nearly all the inhabitants were black. Was it, I wonder, merely coincidence that the only local people we met in the village were all three of them black or were they descendants of Doughty's hosts?

There are many stories to feed the imagination, tales of plague, witches, and treasure at Khaybar. We were surprised by a white horse, appearing without warning, running free through the streets and disappearing as quickly without further sight or sound.

On a more practical level, it might be wise to get permission to wander and photograph in the village from the local Amir's office. The men we met made it clear that that is what we should have done and, furthermore, made us as little welcome as did the Khaybara of Doughty's day.

Of the Khaybar dams, there are two large ones still surviving, Sadd Hasid and Sadd Qasr al-Bint (or al-Qasaybah) - and several smaller ones. They are said to be pre-Islamic and are of stepped construction, like the Sadd Samallagi, near Taif. Sadd Hasid has an arched sluice gate, water conduit and small collecting tank. The tops of the large dams are so wide that *"two horsemen riding over might pass each other"*, in Doughty's phrase.

Sadd Qasr al-Bint is one of the largest ancient dams in the Kingdom. Although it has been breached for about one third of its length, it is nevertheless an impressive 20 metres high and about 135 metres long. The upstream face is plastered with yellow mortar, and the downstream face with bare stone. On the downstream western end is the remains of a large structure, thought to have been some sort of sluice system or additional reservoir.

There is now a reasonable track across the harra to Sadd Qasr al-Bint. To get down into the wadi bed and into the shade of the dhoum palms for a good camping site is slightly more hazardous. There is a track, albeit bumpy with boulders, down into the upstream wadi bed, but those wanting to camp downstream must bump further over the harra until the wadi sides are less steep and a way down can be found. Here, away from the dam, there is no chance of being overlooked by any sightseers and it is quiet and peaceful amongst the acacias and dhoum palms, often with running water in the wadi.

The Khaybar Dam

DIRECTIONS ▶

Jeriat Bishr, Old Khaybar village. The distance from the outskirts of Jeddah to Khaybar village is about 550 km. With a couple of breaks for petrol and lunch, it takes approximately 7 hours.

From Jeddah take the Medina road, by-pass Medina and continue as for Tabuk. New Khaybar is on the main road, about 19 km beyond Thamed.

Turn left into new Khaybar and follow the road north-west, which brings you down into the old village of Khaybar, Jeriat Bishr.

Sadd Qasr al-Bint (or al-Qasaybah). Sadd Qasr al-Bint is approximately 25 km south of Khaybar village. Coming from the direction of Jeddah on the Tabuk road, about 22 km north of Silsilah and 10 km south of the mosque in the centre of Thamud, watch carefully and you will see a track, which has recently been partly asphalted, leading off a lay-by on the eastern side of the road. Follow this track for 2 km and it leads you to the top of the dam.

To get into the wadi upstream of the dam, there is a rough boulder-strewn track from near the top of the dam or another gentler track leads from the road 0.3 km south of the partly asphalted track.

To get into the wadi downstream of the dam is a little more difficult!

It is probably advisable to return to the road and drive about 1 km north (on the west side of the road you may see a rusty old abandoned lorry water tank). Look on the east side for a track and, with luck, it will take you over the harra to the edge of the wadi cliff at a point where you can drive down.

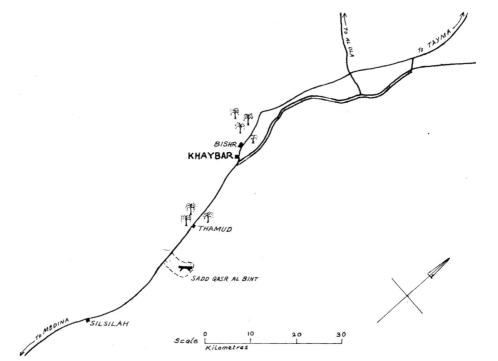

Old Khaybar village

7 Medain Saleh

3-4 DAY TRIP (3-4 nights)

2 WHEEL DRIVE

Many have heard of Petra, the "rose red city half as old as time", the Nabataean city in southern Jordan. But few outside Saudi Arabia know of its complex of sister "cities", Medain Saleh, and fewer still are fortunate enough to have the opportunity of seeing what remains of them. It is an opportunity not to be missed.

Medain Saleh, the cities of Saleh, in ancient times known as Hegra, or by its Arabic name al Hijr, lie in glorious isolation about 845 km from Jeddah in northwest Saudi Arabia, between Tabuk and Medina. Legend has it, sanctified in the Koran, that Saleh was a pre-Islamic prophet, whose word was disbelieved by the inhabitants of the cities of Saleh with the result that they were destroyed by a bolt from heaven in retribution.

Nabataean tombs at Medain Saleh

Fortunately no modern settlement has encroached upon the remains of Medain Saleh. They stand alone in an undulating sea of sand, with islands of weathered sandstone rocks, eroded and rippled into fantastic sculptural shapes. It is into some of these that the Nabateans carved their monumental tombs, a Herculean task when one considers the tons of rock removed to straighten the high facades as they worked from top to bottom.

The area was previously occupied by the Lihyanites, who ruled Dedan. The Nabateans extended their kingdom south from Petra and probably settled here around the beginning of the first century BC.

The Nabateans, originally a nomadic people, were a monarchical society, although sources suggest the kings maintained a structure of consent and consultation with their people. Regional governors were sometimes members of the royal family.

Evidence suggests they worshipped many gods, but their supreme deity was Dushara. Niches containing small stone pillars, or betyls, constituting a shrine to the god Dushara can be seen in the Jebel Ithlib, the group of rocky summits surrounding a central hollow, lying to the north-east of the site. Dushara has neither face nor image. He was a spiritual being, not portrayed in human form, although his throne (or possibly an altar) can be seen in the Jebel Ithlib.

The Nabateans prospered by levying huge tolls on the rich merchandise of the ancient caravans, above all those carrying incense for the Roman Empire from Yemen and Dhofar, whose routes ran through Hejaz. It wasn't until ship-building and navigation advanced and the Red Sea and the Gulf provided an alternative route for the traders from southern Arabia and the East, that Nabatean prosperity began to decline. That was towards the end of the first century AD.

As the name, cities of Saleh, and the size of the site, 9 km^2, suggest, there must have been a sizeable population living here. The extensive area beween the tombs is largely unexcavated, so here may lie the foundations of houses, temples, caravanserais, or a citadel. The stones and material used to build these may have been re-used by succeeding generations, but fortunately for us no one could appropriate the temples or the Jebel Ithlib, carved out of the living rock.

There are about 80 monumental tombs, mostly carved in groups out of the rocky outcrops, of which the Qasr al Bint is of particular interest. Here, one huge tomb has been started and abruptly abandoned, carved down only to the top pediment. Another tomb, the al Farid stands alone, covering a single rock, facing the setting sun. Details

of decoration include capitals and pediments in the style of Greece and Rome, some with a double row of pilasters, many with triglyphs and rosettes, solar discs, urns, snakes, a few masks, griffins and eagles. Nearly all the eagles have had their heads knocked off, one supposes by pious Islamic reformers. The inverted five-step pyramid design, a distinctive feature of Nabatean tomb architecture, crowns many of the tombs.

Medain Saleh is particularly important for its extensive and instructive inscriptions. There are inscriptions on 34 tombs, giving information on ownership, rights of burial, legal details, occasional curses on any who might violate the tomb or fines for those altering the provisions of the inscription. The status of the owner, and the names of family and relations entitled to be buried therein, are often marked. Some are dated to the year of a certain Nabatean king and some carry the names of the masons who carved them.

Inside, the tombs are simple, roughly hewn chambers, still bearing the marks of the chisel, with rectangular burial niches, of varying sizes, cut into the walls. The small ones could have been used for children and possibly as ossuaries to make room for the recent dead. Some tombs have graves sunk into the floor.

When Charles Doughty, the intrepid English traveller, went to Medain Saleh in 1876-7, there were still human bones and remains of linen shrouds from the mummified bodies: *"I saw the sand floor full of rotten clouts, shivering in every wind and taking them up, I found them to be those dry bones' grave-clothes!"*

An engine shed at Medain Saleh

The doors of the tombs were most probably made of wood, acacia or tamarisk timber and, in Doughty's words, "*doubtless have been long since consumed at the cheerful watchfires of the nomads.*"

Jabal Ithlib, the pinnacles of rock standing dramatically on the sky-line to the north-east, surround an open space, which is approached through a narrow gorge called, as in Petra, the Siq. At the outside opening of the Siq is a large open hall cut into the rock, flanked by a pair of pilasters, with stone benches running round the three inside walls. According to Doughty, there had been an architrave, which had fallen with the front of the ceiling. This chamber is the Diwan, thought to have been used for sacred banquets or religious congregations. It must have been pleasantly cool, facing north, the sun never shining in and *"a cool wind breathes there continually"*. The religious significance is suggested by the cult figures and niches with religious inscriptions carved here and on the rocks of the open space inside the Jabal Ithlib. Here is a profound feeling of peace and tranquillity and it is deeply awe-inspiring.

From a rock high on the Jabal Ithlib, called appropriately the "high place", one has a magnificent view over Medain Saleh. About half a mile away to the north-west can be seen the old "kella" or fort, where Doughty stayed in the 1870s, built to protect the water cistern for the pilgrims on their way south to Medina and Makkah. Beside it is the much more recent Turkish station on the famous Hejaz railway built in the first decade of this century.

In the 1980s the "kella", part of which was in danger of collapsing, was dismantled and reconstructed by a Scottish restoration company and the now dry water cistern was patched and replastered. The result is they still stand, but look disappointingly new and lacking in romance, as do the 90-year-old railway station and engine shed of the short-lived Hejaz railway. Inside the shed, however, a sense of romance returns when one sees one of the old steam railway engines used by the Turks, a survivor of the Arab Revolt rallied by T.E. Lawrence.

To gain entrance to the site of Medain Saleh and the al Hijr station, one must obtain a letter of permission from the Department of Antiquities and Museums in Riyadh (*see page 4*).

Al Ula

If time permits on the way to or from Medain Saleh, a short stop at al Ula is highly recommended. Wadi al Ula, 20 km south of Medain Saleh, is a spectacular gorge, green with date palms, running between high red sandstone cliffs.

Here, 2 km north of the modern town, are the ruins of the Khuraybah (Arabic for "ruins"), the ancient capital of the kingdom of Dedan, which flourished in the first millenium BC. Inscriptions indicate the Dedanites were preceded by a Minean settlement, spreading from Yemen. The red sandstone cliffs overlooking the ruins of Khuraybah are pitted with simple square Minean tombs, among them the famous lion tombs. The images of a pair of lions are cut into the rock above the entrance of two tombs.

The museum in al Ula is worth a visit. It displays artefacts dating from early Aramaic and Arab settlements to the Ottoman periods, and of bedouin life. Of special interest, after a visit to Medain Saleh, is a rare example of an undefaced Nabatean miniature eagle's head.

DIRECTIONS

From Jeddah, take the road to Medina. SET YOUR ODOMETER AT **0** at the northern perimeter of Jeddah International Airport.

At Medina follow the by-pass and continue north towards Tabuk. About 15 km from Medina, look to your left and you should see the embankment of the Hejaz railway running parallel to the road. At about 20 km, the old station of al Hafirah comes into view.

Continue on the Tabuk road through Silsilah. At approximately 525 km from Jeddah, 22 km north of Silsilah, you may like to turn off the road and follow the track to the right over the lava fields, to camp by the Khaybar dam (*see trek to Khaybar*).

At 25 km further you pass through Khaybar and approximately 26 km beyond Khaybar, turn left for al Ula.

Follow this road for about 130 km until the road turns left to al Ula and right to Tabuk. Take the Tabuk turn to the right. It's possible to go through al Ula, but the route described above takes you through a beautiful, dramatic landscape of eroded sandstone rocks.

After a further 15 km or so, at the crossroads where the road goes left to al Ula and right to Tabuk, go straight on for Medain Saleh.

Drive on for about 12 km and look for a sign on the left which reads "To the Antiquities". It unfortunately faces the other way, so you have to look backwards! You are now only 5 km from the entrance to the site. There are plenty of wonderful places to camp within easy distance of the perimeter fence.

You can return via al Ula, in which case, after taking the road from the gate, turn right at the T-junction. You will then be heading for al Ula, about 20 km away. There is one more unsigned T-junction; turn left here and the road brings you into al Ula.

Before you reach al Ula, you may want to take a turn to the left, signposted to Khuraybah, the ancient capital of Dedan. It is only about 1 - 2 km off the road.

Returning to Jeddah from al Ula, you can camp again near Khaybar or further to the south, or drive down the way of the old Hejaz railway, camping amongst the mountains near one of the stations (*see trek to Hejaz railway*).

Campsite at Medain Saleh

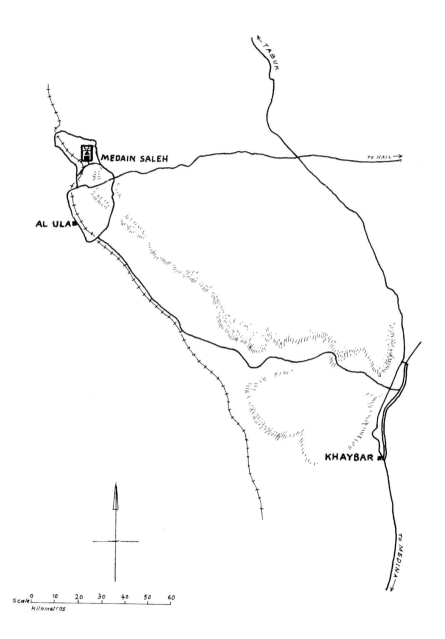

MEDAIN SALEH

AL ULA

KHAYBAR

← TABUK

TO HAIL →

TO MEDINA →

Scale
0 10 20 30 40 50 60
kilometres

25

8 The Hejaz Railway, the final section

3-4 DAY TRIP (3-4 nights)

4 WHEEL
DRIVE

In 1900 Sultan Abdul Hamid of Turkey, the last Caliph, worried by rumblings of Arab discontent, initiated a plan to strengthen the Ottoman hold. The scheme, masterminded by his second secretary, Izzet Pasha, was to build the Hejaz railway from Damascus to the Holy Cities of Medina and Makkah. So, with the declared aim of facilitating the transport of pilgrims, he appealed to the Muslim world for funds. It was built at a cost of £3 million under the direction of the German engineer, Heinrich Meissner, and by 1st September, 1908, the anniversary of the Sultan's accession, it was completed as far as Medina. Although the railway did indeed carry many thousands of pilgrims, it was also a means of moving Turkish troops easily into the heart of Arabia and consolidated the Turkish hold in western Arabia.

From the engineering point of view, building the railway presented few problems in the Hejaz, as it ran over plains and desert and wound between the hills, following the pilgrim's way and the old incense route. The weather, from searing sun and sand storms to unpredictable storms and flash floods, did present a serious hazard. The railway had to be raised on an embankment with over 2,000 bridges and culverts to prevent it being buried in sand or washed away in a flood. However the greatest problem was the hostility of the Arab tribes, who resented the presence of the Christian surveyors, engineers, foremen and labourers too. Not only did they see the railway as an infidel intrusion, but also as a serious threat to their income. Raids on the annual pilgrim caravans was a way of life, which the railway would seriously jeopardize. So railway working parties were constantly under attack from armed bedouin.

By November 1914, Turkey was at war with Britain, France and Russia and in June 1916, the Arab Revolt against Turkish rule finally broke. The British sent officers, such as T.E. Lawrence, ostensibly to help Hussein, the Sharif of Makkah, reclaim Arabia from the Turks. One of the most effective ways of doing so was to cut off the Turks' best means of communication and blow up strategic points of the railway. In the words of Sir Gilbert Clayton of the Arab Bureau, "*The Hejaz railway is the key of the whole problem and it is the permanent cutting of that railway, or at least the dislocation of its running, which is the most important point to aim at.*"

From early 1917 until the fall of Damascus in 1918, Arabs continued to disrupt the railway - without putting it out of action entirely - assisted by the Allies, including men expert in demolition and explosives, such as Garland and also Lawrence, whose affinity with and commitment to the Arab cause was profound. Thereby they kept the maximum number of Turks relatively helpless and distracted from their prime garrisoning and defensive role.

After the war the railway continued to operate spasmodically, but political turmoil in the Hejaz, the cost of repairs due to continual rain and storm damage, and competition from road and finally air travel, made it uneconomic to repair and maintain.

Today almost none of the steel rails or the sleepers remain, tho latter having long since been used by local people as fuel, fencing and props, and the former sold for scrap. Yet much of the embankment and all the culverts and bridges are still there

Still standing impressively every 20 kilometres or so are the stations, water towers and Turkish barracks and forts. The forts are sturdily built of sandstone or black basalt with external windows serving as gun slits. The double water towers with their stone shield against sniper fire, together with the garrison buildings, occur every three or four stations.

As well as the steam locomotive standing in the repair workshop at the station at Medain Saleh, there are still derailed locomotives, coal tenders and wagons to be seen at Tuwayrah, Wayban, Hadiyah and al Buwayr stations.

At al Mudaraj, or Mudowwara, are Turkish graves, presumably those of the soldiers who died when Lawrence and his bedouin blew up a double-engined train, between here and Hadiyah. Lawrence has recorded: " *Accordingly, when the front 'driver' of the second engine was on the bridge, I raised my hand to Salem. There followed a terrific roar, and the line vanished from sight behind a spouting column of black dust and smoke a hundred feet high and wide.* "

Driving the approximate 150 km of railway between Qa'alat Zumurrud and al Buwayr is sometimes hard going and requires constant attention. The embankment will often end abruptly in a hole, or narrow alarmingly to barely the width of your vehicle, or else large tracts of it will disappear, swept away by wind or water. At one point a huge sand dune blocks your way and at another a rock fall obstructs your passage. Always do a *recce* of any difficult-looking terrain, particularly as there are frequent hidden hazards.

Listen for far-away storms in the mountains. We were once caught out and met a flash flood sweeping up the wadi, like the sea surging up a creek.

The choice of camping places is unlimited, although it is wise to choose slightly high ground. There is much magnificent, wild and savage country, far from roads and permanent habitation. It is a journey with a *frisson* of excitement and a trail of romantic history, from the ancient frankincense and myrrh traders, to the huge caravans of Hajj pilgrims, to remnants of the Ottoman Empire soldiers steaming south to Medina, to T.E. Lawrence and his like with their wild armies of bedouin fighting their way north.

DIRECTIONS

Take the Medina road out of Jeddah. By-pass Medina and continue on the Tabuk road towards Khaybar.

There are several possibilities for this trek. If you can afford the time, we suggest a 3 or even 4 night trip, camping first at the Khaybar dam (*see trek to Khaybar*), next at Medain Saleh (*see trek to Medain Saleh*) and then one night on the Hejaz railway or better still two nights, which would allow time to linger in al Ula and Khuraybah.

From al Ula, SET YOUR ODOMETER AT **0**. Take the Medina road south. At about 80 km turn off the road to the right near a microwave dish and join the railway just before Zumurrud station.

If you have 4 nights, you can make your first camp somewhere near the next station, Sawrah, and your final camp further down the line and have an easy run home to Jeddah, having rejoined the Medina road 85 km north-west of Medina.

If you have just 3 nights, we suggest you camp near Hadiyah station, from where it should be about a 10 hour drive of approximately 600 km. back to Jeddah.

The 150 kilometres of cross-country railway can be covered in 9-10 hours.

The Hejaz Railway

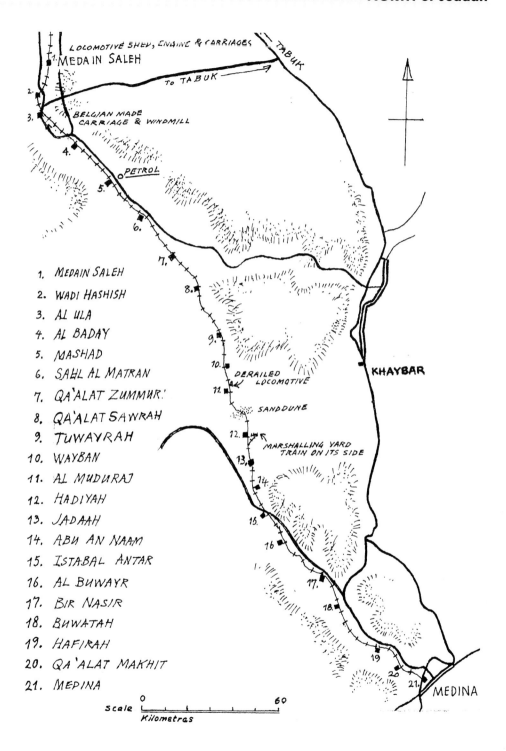

1. MEDAIN SALEH
2. WADI HASHISH
3. AL ULA
4. AL BADAY
5. MASHAD
6. SAHL AL MATRAN
7. QA'ALAT ZUMMUR.
8. QA'ALAT SAWRAH
9. TUWAYRAH
10. WAYBAN
11. AL MUDURAJ
12. HADIYAH
13. JADAAH
14. ABU AN NAAM
15. ISTABAL ANTAR
16. AL BUWAYR
17. BIR NASIR
18. BUWATAH
19. HAFIRAH
20. QA'ALAT MAKHIT
21. MEDINA

Scale
0   60
Kilometras

9 Tabuk and Tayma

3-4 DAY TRIP (3-4 nights)

2 WHEEL DRIVE **4** WHEEL DRIVE

Tabuk, 1100 km north of Jeddah and now a busy metropolis, was once a traditional stopping place for tribes migrating from Yemen to summer pastures in Jordan and Syria. Here it is said the Prophet Mohammed found a fresh water spring.

In order to pack as much as possible into a precious Eid holiday, we cheated a little on this trek by putting our vehicle onto a lorry going to Tabuk and then flying up to collect it and then to provision it at a local supermarket, before beginning our exploratory trip southwards towards Jeddah.

Before leaving Tabuk, we looked briefly at the old Turkish fort, dating from 1694 AD, and at the Turkish railway station, the biggest one built on the old Hejaz line. Both have been so carefully restored that they look almost new!

There is of course much to see around Tabuk that is not included here. We were limited to 3 or 4 days, so we at once took the road south-east to Tayma, 255 km away.

Tayma lies in an oasis, surrounded by a wide stretch of arid desert. Watered by the great and inexhaustible well, Bir Haddaj, it has been inhabited since the days of the Midianites in the late Bronze Age.

Tayma was in a strategic position at the junction of trade routes running north, south, east and west. It connected the Holy places of the Hejaz with the Mediterranean littoral.

The antiquities of Tayma are among the earliest and most significant of north-west Arabia. The ruins of the old city spread for miles and are surrounded by the ancient city wall, said to have been about 7 km in circumference. Much of it still stands and is preserved in places to a height of 4 metres.

About 550 BC Nabonidus, the last king of the neo-Babylonians, moved his imperial seat here from Babylon. According to an inscription found in Turkey and ascribed to the king himself, he made the town beautiful and built himself a palace equal to his palace in Babylon. This, and much else built by him, is reputed still to lie beneath the ruins of the city.

Later Tayma came under Nabatean rule. It declined in importance when, because of the shifting routes, the Islamic pilgrims started to avoid it.

The famous Tayma stones, inscribed in the Aramaic of two millenia or longer ago, now in the Louvre, were found here in 1884 by the Alsatian naturalist, Huber. The Qasr al-Hamra Cube, now in the museum in Riyadh, is another antiquity of Tayma. Both show religious symbols of Mesopotamian origin.

Thousands of inscriptions in the pre-Islamic Thamudic script have been found in the surrounding area of Tayma as well as in the city itself. About 10 miles south-east of the town is a solitary hill called Jabal Ghunaim, and here St. John Philby, the English explorer and friend of King Abdul Aziz, found inscriptions thought to be the earliest yet discovered in north Arabia in Thamudic script. They record wars that may have been waged by Nabonidus and show several faces of the deity, Salm, personal name inscriptions and pictures of camels.

Coming from the direction of Tabuk on the left-hand side of the road, just outside the old city wall, is the Tayma museum, which houses many of the archaeological finds.

On the same side, just inside the city wall, is the Qasr ar-Radam, the best preserved building, originally built in the first millenium BC. There are some Thamudic inscriptions to be seen here. The Bir Haddaj, the enormous well and a source of water for more than two and a half thousand years, today stands in the middle of a quiet round-about in the town.

Nearby is the old Amir's fort, which, although of far less historic significance in comparison to the more ancient antiquities of Tayma, is nonetheless a fascinating place to explore. To get in, you must climb through a small door set in the big entrance gate. Once inside, you will find a warren of passages, small rooms, a tall pillared hall, an inner courtyard, and stairways leading to upper floors and the roof.

The desert immediately around Tayma seems flat and rather exposed, but to the north-west are some pleasant hills with at least one lovely peaceful wadi in which to camp. However there is not much wood for burning even though there are a number of attractive living trees, so it is advisable to bring wood or charcoal with you. The hills enclosing the wadi and the sand-filled gorges are a good gentle climb in the cool of the morning. Look over the hills, stretching far to the west, and imagine the Hejaz railway winding its way south to Medain Saleh.

The Bir Haddaj

31

DIRECTIONS

There are several companies that transport cars to Tabuk at a cost, at the time of writing, of 300 to 400 riyals.

From Tabuk take the Tayma/Medina road south 255 km to Tayma.

For night one, the wadi campsite north-west of Tayma, take the Tabuk road north again. SET YOUR ODOMETER AT **0** at the police checkpoint on the outskirts of Tayma. At 39 km, turn off the road onto a track running west towards some low hills. Follow the track until you are in a quiet sandy wadi between the hills approximately 16 km from the road.

Night two by Medain Saleh: from Tayma take the Medina road south for approximately 110 km and turn right to al Ula. Drive for about 95 km and turn right again to Medain Saleh. Drive on until you reach a sign, facing the other way, reading "To the antiquities", in about 12 km. Remember, to see the ruins of Medain Saleh, you must have the appropriate letter of permission *(see page 4)*.

The following day you could visit Khuraybah and al Ula, 20 km south of Medain Saleh *(see directions Medain Saleh)*.

Night three could be spent on the Hejaz railway. Follow the road south from al Ula for about 79 km, stopping for petrol at 39 km. Join the railway near the microwave dish *(see directions Hejaz railway)*.

Alternatively night three could be spent at Sad Qasr al-Bint, the great dam 25 km south of Khaybar. From al Ula drive on south to Khaybar, continue for 25 km and turn left off the road to the dam *(see directions Khaybar dam)*. The journey back to Jeddah from Khaybar takes about 7 hours, including coffee, lunch and petrol stops.

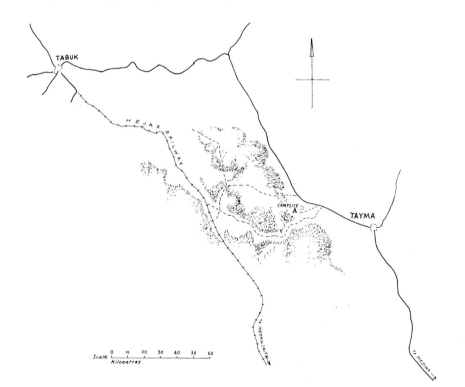

10 Rabigh Beach

DAY OR WEEKEND TRIP (2 hrs)

4 WHEEL DRIVE

Rabigh beach is a long quiet stretch of sand about 150 km north of Jeddah. It is a good place to camp with children and is excellent for swimming, snorkelling and diving. As at Shuwaiba, the reef is alive with a multitude of life, brilliant coral and shimmering shoals of fish, darting in and out of the reef.

It lies to the west of Rabigh, which at the present day appears to be a thriving town. Rabigh is often mentioned in the early part of T.E. Lawrence's "Seven Pillars of Wisdom", as it was of strategic importance at the beginning of the Arab Revolt. It was the sea base for incoming stores and arms shipped from Suez. While the Turks still held Medina, it was feared they might try to recapture Makkah. Rabigh, lying half-way between Medina and Makkah, was therefore well garrisoned and supplied, to guard against such an attack. As the Arabs gained ground and captured the port of Wedj, so Rabigh diminished in importance.

The beach is pleasantly isolated and well guarded by the coast guards. To get there you must pass their checkpoint, where they scrupulously examine iqamas or passports, and travel letters, keeping the former until you return. If you want to dive, take your dive card or proof of qualification, which they may ask to see. They sometimes forbid video cameras. If you abide by the rules, they are friendly and allow you to camp where you like.

The reef is beautiful, and the land pleasant, although the land behind is aptly described by T.E. Lawrence as *"the sandy and featureless strip of desert bordering the Western coast of Arabia between sea-beach and littoral hills, for hundreds of monotonous miles."* The rather dreary drive up the coast tends to confirm this, but, once on the beach, the sand is wonderfully white and the sea exquisitely turquoise and blue. It is ideal for small children in the sandy shallows and for older children and adults to snorkel or dive. There is some exciting diving through a narrow tunnel of coral into a clear lagoon at the northern end of the beach.

For the non-swimmers, there are plenty of lovely shells and little pieces of red and white coral washed up on the beach to collect, and a number of sea birds to watch.

As at Shuwaiba, take an awning or tent for shade. There is usually some driftwood for a fire.

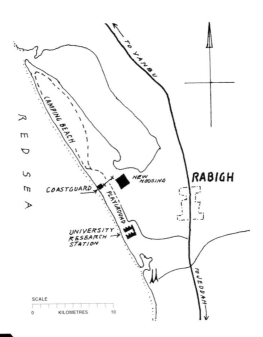

Take the Medina road north out of Jeddah. SET YOUR ODOMETER AT 0 at the junction with the ring road expressway, the al Haramain road and the Medina or al Munawwarah road. There is a police checkpoint just after this junction. Continue northwards for about 54 km. Turn left for Thuwal, Qadimah and Rabigh. At 56 km turn right to Qadimah and Rabigh. Turn left for Thuwal, Qadimah and Rabigh. At 105 km you will pass the right turn to Johfah. When you reach 115 km as you approach a small town or suburb of Rabigh, there is a large blue sign written in Arabic, directions to the refinery on the left. You must turn off the road to the right, down into a dip and turn left to go under the road. Ahead of you are the gates leading into the refinery. Turn right immediately before them, following a sign to "The Community, 19 km".

Drive straight on past a roundabout at 125 km still following signs to "The Community", past the gates of the University Research Station and round to the left at the end of its wall at 128 km, towards the sea.

Follow the coast road, past a long playground and at 131.5 km turn off it onto a well beaten track by the sea and ahead of you at 134.6 km you will see the Coastguards Post on the left and a large housing compound on the right.

Once through the coastguards checkpoint, you can drive along the coast for about 15 km and choose your campsite. The track is well beaten, but beware of some very soft sand near the sea.

11 **Wadi Turabah**

WEEKEND TRIP (5 hrs)

4 WHEEL
DRIVE

The stretch of Wadi Turabah lying approximately 80 km south of Turabah town is beautiful. Turabah is one of the few wadis in Saudi Arabia with permanently flowing water. Consequently it is rich in wildlife and, near the water, lush with vegetation. There are grassy banks, clumps of tall reeds with feathery tops and bushes of aromatic herbs and sweet smelling mint. The pools are teeming with small brown fish and frogs that jump so far over the water they seem almost to fly. Dragonflies skim the water and butterflies flit between the bushes.

Hump-backed cows, similar to the African cows, wade in the water or graze along the banks. Herds of semi-wild donkeys shyly come to drink the water and families of baboons can sometimes be seen running and clambering up the crags above. Here it is possible to see gazelle too, but, because they are scarce and understandably fearful of man, sightings are rare.

There are long spiny-backed lizards and, we are told, snakes, as well as many varieties of birds: soaring kites, primeval-looking hammercops, elegant egrets and grey herons; as well as smaller birds such as wheatears, shrikes, and kingfishers and bee-eaters, bright flashes of colour above the water.

The water springs from deep wells and runs through the wadi for about 18 km before disappearing underground again. Most of its course is flanked by steep-sided mountains.

Once again one should be warned of bilharzia in the water and should not venture in.

Wadi Turabah is a good 5-hour drive from Jeddah and if, as for so many of us, your weekend doesn't start until 1 pm on Thursday, it is difficult to get far into the wadi before nightfall. Once in the wadi, the going is rough and stony and therefore slow, while the water stream only begins nearly 20 km up the wadi; so you may not reach a suitable grassy platform on the water bank on which to camp. There is, however, an alternative, which we thought was ideal and had the great advantage of being comparatively mosquito-free, at least when we were there in early October: follow the directions up Wadi Turabah for 11.5 km. Where the wadi forks, take the left fork into the slightly narrower Wadi Nakhl. After about 1 km there is a clump of trees on raised ground to the left and an ideal level camping site under a small tree, which provides excellent shade in the morning.

Opposite the camping site on its west side, the rock face rises steeply, but it can be climbed at a more gentle gradient on either flank and is worth the effort. Not only is the view magnificent, but there are also ancient rock graffiti at the peak, close to the edge of the cliff above and slightly south of the camp, consisting of camels, ibex, the front face of a wild oxen and what I was told are probably wasm or tribal territorial marks.

Back in Wadi Turabah, drive on through the narrowing wadi and within a few kilometres the water appears. The track follows the stream, crossing and recrossing many times. Frequent stops are irresistible.

Rounding Jebel Ibrahim, the wadi brings one to a bewildering number of misleading tracks, but the most beaten one finally leads onto the al Baha/Bani Saad road. The road back towards Taif via Bani Saad is an easy but spectacular run through dark mountain tunnels and over breathtaking viaducts affording glimpses of the wonderful views from the edge of the escarpment.

Wadi Turabah

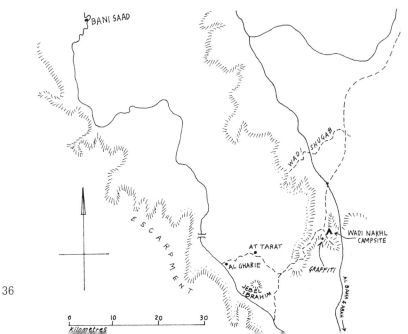

Leave Jeddah by the Makkah road. SET YOUR ODOMETER AT **0** by the green palm sculpture at the junction of the expressway and al Falah Street.

At 38 km turn right onto the non-Muslim road and follow the road leading to Taif up the escarpment.

Continue towards Taif and at 160 km turn right for Riyadh at an Exit sign and a green sign for the Massarah Intercontinental Hotel. The road sweeps up and round onto the by-pass. Follow it for about 7 km, until you reach a T junction under a flyover. Turn right.

Drive just 1.5 km and turn left at the traffic lights and a sign reading "Obligatory road for trucks".

Follow this road round, and bear left in a little over 0.5 km. Continue on the King Khalid ring road, until you reach the T junction at the Taif/Abha road at odometer reading 178 km. Turn left towards Abha.

At about 266 km you will see the left turn to Turabah. Drive on past it until, at 304 km, you see a sign reading "Wadi Turabah" just before a bridge. Take the track leading off the road to the right and down into the wadi. SET YOUR ODOMETER AT **0.**

Follow the track which runs beside a wire-mesh fence. When the fence finishes, continue on the track in a south-westerly direction up the wadi. At about 3 km bear left into the river-bed at a fork in the track. At the next fork, at 4 km, bear right. Follow the main wadi until, at 11.5 km, the wadi itself forks. The slightly wider wadi to the right is Wadi Turabah and the one to the left is Wadi Nakhl. SET YOUR ODOMETER AT **0.** In less than 1 km, on the left up Wadi Nakhl, under a tall tree, is a good flat camping site on slightly raised ground.

Alternatively, if you have time and light, you may wish to continue up Wadi Turabah and find a camping site near the water. There are several attractive places on high grass banks on the east side away from the track and shaded from the rising sun in the morning.

To reach the Abha/Bani Saad road, continue along Wadi Turabah (you have already set your odometer at **0** at the junction with Wadi Nakhl). At 17.6 km fork right, cross the water and follow the track into the right hand wadi. The tracks now become confused, but follow the most beaten track and you find yourself gradually heading north-west. Jebel Ibrahim, a beautiful bluish mountain, rises above the others to your left. At 29.5 km you reach the first village, which may be At Taraf. Leave it on your right and again follow the most beaten tracks past more villages. Finally the track leads you onto the al Baha/Bani Saad road. Turn right to Bani Saad, on to Taif and so back to Jeddah.

12 Shuwaiba Beach

DAY OR WEEKEND TRIP (1½ - 2 hrs)

2 WHEEL DRIVE   **4** WHEEL DRIVE

Shuwaiba is an area of beach and lagoons on the coast to the south of Jeddah. In 646 AD it was considered as a possible landing place for pilgrims coming by sea to Makkah. Caliph Uthman, however, decided that Jeddah was more appropriate, being less vulnerable to pirates.

Its easy proximity to Jeddah makes it a popular picnic and camping place. The white sandy bottom of the shallows leading out to the reef is a near perfect playground for small children, provided they wear shoes, but beware of the litter strewn over the shore.

The reef is easily accessible and is excellent for snorkelling and diving. Among the myriads of brilliant fish in the reef, we have swum here with turtles and seen beautiful blue spotted rays.

At night millions of crabs run busily over the beach and if you are a shell collector, have a heart for the tiny hermit crabs who make some of the prettiest shells their home by day.

It is essential to take some kind of awning, as there is no shade whatsoever. If you want a fire, bring your own firewood for you will be lucky to find more than the occasional piece of driftwood.

The coastguards are quite vigilant and drive up and down the coast at intervals throughout the night. Occasionally they are inclined to drop in to your camp, driven, one suspects, more by curiosity or boredom than suspicion.

DIRECTIONS ▸

Take the Makkah road from Jeddah. SET YOUR ODOMETER AT **0** by
the green palm sculpture at the junction of the expressway, al
Haramain Road and al Falah Street. At about 39 km, before the
"Muslim only" checkpoint, turn right onto the by-pass south of
Makkah. Just after the Haj bus depot on the left is a petrol station and
the turn to Gizan and al Lith. Take this turn, SET YOUR ODOMETER
AT **0** and continue for 43 km until the next police checkpoint.

Here, just before the checkpoint, you can fork right and head south-
west for "Closed" Shuwaiba or you can continue straight on through
the checkpoint and turn right after 2 km. "Closed" Shuwaiba is slightly closer to Jeddah and therefore tends to be more populated, which is
why we usually recommend turning right 2 km past the checkpoint.
This road follows a line of pylons leading to a desalination plant. At
the desalination plant, follow around the outside of the boundary wall
to the right until you reach the sea. Then right again and up the coast
until you find a suitable camping or picnic spot.

Alternatively, follow the boundary wall to the left and about
2 or 3 km south of the desalination plant is a lagoon, suitable for
windsurfing.

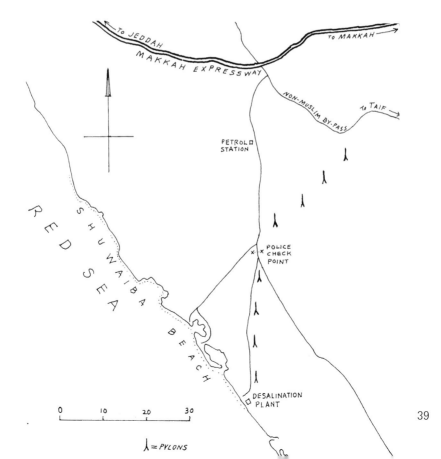

39

13 The Hot Springs at Wadi al Lith

WEEKEND TRIP (3-3½ hrs)

2 WHEEL DRIVE

Happily, at the time of writing, no tarmac road penetrates into Wadi al Lith further than Ghumayqah. Therefore the hot springs, although well-known, are not crowded with visitors, as one might imagine, particularly in the light of the medicinal reputation of the waters. Once on the track from Ghumayqah, it is an easy albeit stony road, interspersed with patches of sand, but wide and clear. It rises and falls over shallow rocky hills for about 19 km until, near the springs, it reaches a hamlet boasting a surprisingly large school.

Here, by the track, is a green sign in Arabic directing you to "the hot waters", about 0.5 km away. As you move towards the wadi centre, a delightful stretch of swiftly running water is now revealed. Until you paddle into the shallows, there is no indication that this is different from any other clear, enchanting wadi stream. In fact, there is no way of knowing where the springs are until you enter the water. Once in, however, a step in one direction and hot water is rippling around your foot; a step in another direction and you are back in a cool current.

Further upstream on the near side are pleasant grassy banks and clumps of high reeds, egrets and hammerkops wading in the shallows and small brown fish darting through the deeper pools. Some in our party peered through binoculars, identifying birds, while others explored further afield or gazed at the tranquil scene of resting camels and grazing donkeys on the far bank; but one optimistic member waded into the stream with his fishing rod and cast his fly over the water. I think the fish must have been so surprised by such eccentric behaviour that it never occurred to them to take a bite.

The wadi is wide at this point and the surrounding mountains rise steadily to the great escarpment, which reaches a height of over 8000 ft. It is wonderfully untamable country, demanding awe and respect.

Fly-fishing at Wadi al Lith

DIRECTIONS

Take the Makkah road out of Jeddah. SET YOUR ODOMETER AT **0** by the palm sculpture at the junction of the expressway and al Falah Street.

Turn right onto the non-Muslim by-pass at 38 km and right again at 40 km onto the Gizan road. Follow this road straight on through the police checkpoint at 80 km until you reach the al Lith crossroads at 205 km. Turn left to Ghumayqah. RESET YOUR ODOMETER AT **0**.

At 26 km, where there is a mini-roundabout, drive straight on, even though the sign to Ghumayqah directs you left. In less than 1 km, when you are in the village, the road bends sharply round to the left. Leave the road right on the corner, on a track going straight on towards a large yellow building, the local school. Turn right directly in front of the school, following the track which takes you around it, leaving it to your left.

Now follow the track straight on for about 19 km. At 46 km you will see another large schoolhouse ahead of you on the right. Here there is another fork in the road. A green sign, written in Arabic, points left to the hot springs less than 1 km away over the wadi.

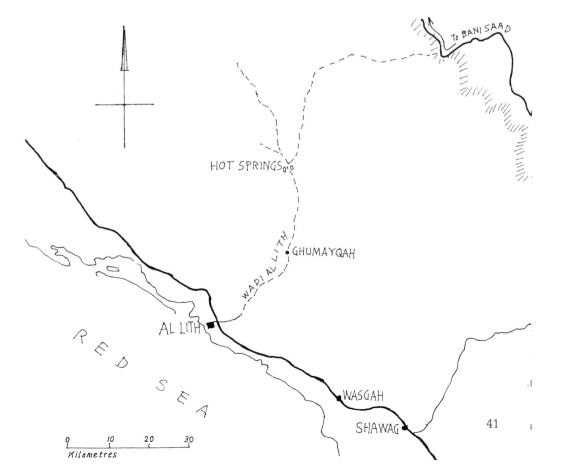

41

14 Wadi Ilyab

WEEKEND TRIP (3-3½ hrs)

4 WHEEL DRIVE

South of al Lith, near the road leading east to Adam al Hulay, there is an easily accessible wide wadi meandering down from the mountains. After the harsh, flat, bleached landscape, which borders the coastal road for mile after monotonous mile, Wadi Ilyab is a pleasant relief. With running water, shrubs luxuriant with pale green foliage and a backdrop of dark mountains, the soft muted colours give it an appearance of a cool oasis. Cool it is not, particularly in summer, but in late autumn, winter and spring it is a good place to go to watch the wildlife.

In springtime, we are told, many baby camels are born here. Baboons scuttle away at the approach of humans, unlike their brothers on the al Hada escarpment road, who grow fat on their booty from man *(see trek to Wadi Uranah)*.

Birds are attracted to the water of Wadi Ilyab to feed off the fish and small frogs, the insects skimming over the water, and the berries of the *salvatore persica* in the autumn.

In the sandbanks are holes and burrows suggesting nocturnal animals. It is wise to tread carefully at night to avoid the occasional snake.

When we went to camp, we drove across the water and up into a side wadi in order to be further from the road and away from the water, with its mosquitoes and sandflies. Here was that wonderful stillness of a desert night, where "the night crept in on feet of fur".

In the morning there are flaky peaks to be climbed, from which to admire the view. There is little shade, so it is not a place to linger late into the morning without a tent.

Wadi Ilyab

DIRECTIONS

Leave Jeddah by the Makkah road. SET YOUR ODOMETER AT **0** by the palm sculpture at the junction of the expressway and al Falah Street.

At 38 km turn right onto the non-Muslim by-pass. At 40 km turn right again towards Gizan. Go straight on past the checkpoint at 80 km and again at 205 km at the al Lith turning.

Drive straight through Wasqah at 240 km and Shawag at 260 km. Turn left 2 km beyond Shawag, following the sign to Adam. RE-SET YOUR ODOMETER AT **0**. Follow this road for 27 km.

Turn off the road to the left and you will find you are in Wadi Ilyab with the water running down the middle about 0.5 km away.

You can camp in the wadi or, as we did, drive through the water and up a side wadi for about 6 km to a campsite on a raised bank amongst the acacias. There is plenty of firewood to be found.

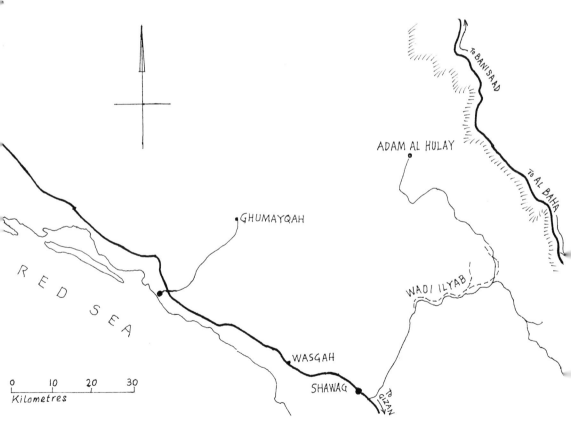

15 **Wadi Sadiyah**

WEEKEND TRIP (3 hrs)

4 WHEEL
DRIVE

This quiet, secluded site lies in a small wadi enclosed on three sides by high
rocky crags.The entrance is sometimes almost entirely obscured by densely
growing *calotropis procera* or sodom apples. Even before these grew so tall, one
could easily miss the opening while driving down the wide sweep of Wadi
Sadiyah, were it not for a distinctive landmark. High on the rocks overlooking
the entrance is the ruin of an old Turkish look-out post.

Once inside the side wadi there is a sweep of soft sand and, as you wind
your way through the acacias, it opens out onto firmer ground, bordered by large
smooth rocks.

If you arrive in the late afternoon,you will have chosen the perfect time for an
undemanding climb up to the Turkish look-out post, from which you have a fine
view up and down the main wadi and of the sun going down behind the mountains.

The longer, higher climb up the mountain at the end of the little wadi is a
rewarding one to make before breakfast, before it is too hot. In the soft and
muted light of the early morning, the magnificent view over the mountains, the
wadis and the pin-sized camp below (where with any luck someone has stayed
behind to prepare breakfast) is stunning.

Close to the campsite, on the left-hand side as you face the back of the wadi,

some interesting graffiti are pecked into the rocks
above *(see inset)*. These are thought to be around
2000 years old. Camels and oryx are clearly recog-
nisable amongst the figures.

On our first visit there was water running in
Wadi Sadiyah. After dinner we walked out into
the main wadi, following the croak of the toads to
find, in the beam of our torches, hundreds of them
and thousands of little tadpoles in the water.
However one should take care, as it is surprisingly difficult to find one's way back into the side
wadi in the dark!

Of the other wildlife, we have seen camel spi-
ders, bats, little mice, praying mantis, lizards, a scorpion, a hedgehog, an
Imperial eagle, an Egyptian vulture, bulbuls and other small birds. One may be
woken by wandering camels in the morning and later, a flock of goats may pass
by on their way up the mountain, stripping bare anything in their path.

Growing high amongst the crags, we saw a particularly fine specimen of
caralluma europaea. Its deep red flowers looked magnificent, but its smell is evil,
like rotting meat, attracting the flies, which pollenate the flowers. Another beauty growing in the big wadi is the poisonous lily.

It is wise to bring wood or collect it on the way if you want a fire, as there is
little to be found at the site.

DIRECTIONS

Take the Makkah road from Jeddah. SET YOUR ODOMETER AT **0** by the green palm sculpture at the junction of the expressway, al Haramain road and al Falah Street. At about 39 km before the "Muslim-only" checkpoint, turn right onto the by-pass and Taif road. Just after the Haj bus depot on the left, turn right onto the Gizan road at 40 km. Follow the Gizan road and when you reach the police checkpoint at 80 km, RE-SET YOUR ODOMETER AT **0**.

At 36 km there is a garage. FILL UP WITH PETROL. Drive straight on until you see a big blue sign: "Al Lith 75 km". About 0.5 km past it, and between two dark hillocks on either side of the road, at odometer reading 48 km, turn left off the road onto an ill-defined track over the desert.

Head north-east at a 45° angle to the road. There is a wide expanse of sand in front of you. Have courage, keep going and after a few kilometres you will find yourself in a long, scattered village of white box-houses and animal enclosures. Pass through, following the track, keeping alert for chickens, goats and children. At about 58.5 km you will notice cultivation to your right. After 1 km bear right down the wadi bed.

Drive up the wadi. At 64 km, keep to the right, low in the wadi in a north-north-easterly direction. At 68.5 km you should see a green sign in Arabic on your left. Beyond this are the few houses and yellow mosque of Sadiyah on the left bank of the wadi. Another 1.8 km brings you to an old well. Beside it on the left is the ruin of a small watchtower. Move to the right side of the wadi and drive for 0.7 km. Bear right up the wadi (there is a well-beaten track which tries to lead you left here). Continue up the wide sandy bed, now with hills on either side, for another 19 km. Keep near the mountains to the right, winding through a forest of *calotropis procera*. Look for the old Turkish watchtower, high on the right. Once abreast of it, turn in towards the rocks and you will find the entrance to the side wadi. Drive up through some soft sand for a few hundred metres and there at the back of the wadi is the ideal camping site.

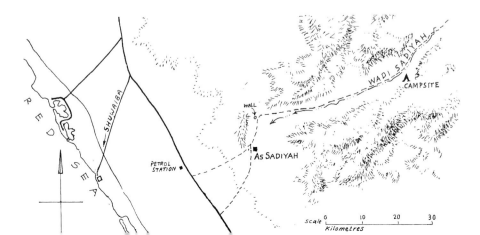

16 The Ancient Dam, Sadd Samallagi

DAY OR WEEKEND TRIP (2½-3 hrs)

2 WHEEL DRIVE   **4** WHEEL DRIVE (campsite)

The substantial remains of Sadd Samallagi are to be found in Wadi Liyya about 25 km south of Taif.

The dam, or sadd, is thought to be pre-Islamic, built at the same time as many of the great Yemeni dams. There is, however, a school of thought suggesting it was built later, in Abbasid times, when much construction work was undertaken, including the famous pools on Darb Zubaida.

Whenever it was built, it is an impressive achievement. It once spanned the wadi, over 200 metres across, from a hill on one side to a rocky outcrop on the other. The latter end was breached, forming a narrow gorge, through which the water must have gushed and where a track now runs from the overlooking village.

The dam is constructed of large, uncut, unmortared boulders, infilled with small stones. The downstream side is steeply stepped and rises about 15 metres to a wide top, approximately 10 metres across. The top is flat and smooth, like a Roman road, and was once finished with plaster, some of which remains.

Overlooking Sadd Samallagi, at each end, are two mintars or watchtowers. One stands alone, high on the hill, and the other on the rocky outcrop now surrounded by the present day village. These watchtowers are excellent landmarks, for in spite of its size the dam is quite difficult to see if one is approaching along the track on the upstream side, where tall acacias block the view.

Downstream, the land is abundantly cultivated. There are vines, pomegranate and fig trees, courgettes and cucumbers, seemingly watered from an old deep well, on the top of which we saw a specimen of Jayakar's agamid lizard. This is a long, exotic and beautiful creature of vivid blue with a broad band of gold circling its tail. It stood proudly as if guarding the well and only moved a foot or two down into the well when approached within touching distance.

The immediate area of Sadd Samallagi is too populated for camping. Although we only saw one man, I think many eyes must have been watching us from the village! However if you return the short distance to the road, on the other side is a rough track leading over the rocky hill and beyond is a quiet and isolated wadi, with some thorn trees for shade. Being high in the hills, the wadi is not too hot for summer camping and indeed can still be quite cold during the hour before dawn.

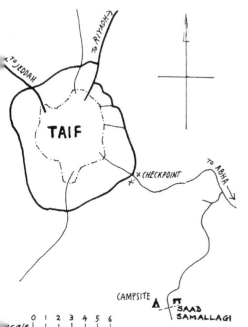

TAIF

To RIYADH

To JEDDAH

To ABHA

CHECKPOINT

CAMPSITE

SAAD SAMALLAGI

scale 0 1 2 3 4 5 6 kilometres

DIRECTIONS

Take the Makkah road from Jeddah. SET YOUR ODOMETER AT **0** by the green palm sculpture at the junction of the expressway, al Haramain Road and al Falah Street. Drive towards Taif via the non-Muslim by-pass south of Makkah. At the top of the escarpment, your odometer should read about 146 km.

You can drive through the centre of Taif and out onto the Abha road or use the following directions round the ring road:

At odometer reading 162 km turn right at an EXIT sign and a sign for the Massarah Intercontinental Hotel. This road sweeps you round and over the road you have just left, in the direction of Riyadh.

Drive straight on until you reach a T-junction under a flyover at about 169 km. Turn right under the flyover onto the main road towards Taif centre. After 1.5 km turn left at the lights. In just over 0.5 km bear left again, where there is a new mini-roundabout, onto King Khalid Road.

Follow this ring road round until you get to traffic lights at a T-junction at 180 km and turn left. There is a checkpoint almost immediately.

You are now on the Abha Road. At 188 km you will see a sign reading "Wadi Liyya". Continue until you see a turn to the right to Tamalah at 189 km.

Turn right to Tamalah and RE-SET YOUR ODOMETER AT **0**.

After 1 km turn left, signposted to Tamalah again.

At 12.8 km there is a white sign with Sadd Samallagi written in Arabic in red and a black arrow pointing to a track on the left.

Follow the track up and over a small hillock towards a village. The track then forks in many directions. Take a track bending right and slightly away from the village, which will take you to the wadi bed. Bend left and here behind some acacias you should find the dam. From the Sadd Samallagi sign on the road, the dam lies in a direct line below the ruin of the largest watchtower on the far hill.

The Ancient Dam

To find the campsite, return to the road. RE-SET YOUR ODOMETER AT **0**.

Take the track on the other side of the road, which leads over the mountain on a very rough track and down the other side into a wadi. Here the track bends left at 1.8 km. If you leave the track and turn right and drive along the wadi bed, you will come to a pleasant campsite shaded by acacias at approximately 2 km from the road.

17 **Bani Saad**

WEEKEND TRIP (4 hrs)

2 WHEEL DRIVE **4** WHEEL DRIVE

Bani Saad lies in the mountains, 8000 ft above sea level, south of Taif. It is a hilly area of old stone villages overlooked by ancient watchtowers. About 17 km beyond Bani Saad there is a turn off the road where a track winds down to a campsite with a view of mountain peaks, sometimes hazy in cloud or a light luminous fog. Between them runs a wadi, about 3000 ft. below, disappearing towards al Lith, 139 km away.

After the heat of the plains at sea level, the cool evening air takes one by surprise and at night it becomes quite cold, so take warm clothes and blankets. It might also be wise to collect wood on the way. Some can be found, but up here it is a precious commodity.

At dawn the sun catches the peaks in turn and slowly moves down the slopes until the wadis below are aflame with sunlight.

On the steep rocky slope amongst the boulders grow clumps of aromatic lavender, sage, whispy tall grasses and juniper. There are also splashes of yellow in dark green foliage and specks of red of flowers unknown to me. Attracted to these are butterflies, a bright little orange one most in evidence.

A day could be spent very pleasantly clambering over the rocks amongst the flowers, bird watching or just relaxing in the welcome cool of the mountains before returning via Taif and down the escarpment road to Jeddah.

There is however an alternative for the intrepid traveller and that is down the steep track leading into the head of Wadi al Lith. From here you have a rough, slow drive for over 100 km through the wadi, until you reach the open desert, a tarmac road, al Lith, the sea and a road back to Jeddah. Consider carefully before you embark on it. In some places the going is extremely slow and difficult, so it takes a minimum of seven hours, *without a stop,* before you reach the tarmac road and a further two-and-a-half hours drive back to Jeddah. Make sure you have a full petrol tank, plenty of water (it is much hotter as soon as you are down in the wadi), spare car parts and tow ropes. One final warning — do not undertake it if there has recently been heavy rainfall in the mountains, as some of the narrow gorges would certainly be impassable.

Having issued dire warnings, I can now say that with enough time, favourable conditions and strong vehicles, it is a journey well worth making.

At first the track drops abruptly and steeply for several thousand feet. On the summit of a lower peak stands an ancient stone watchtower, guarding the entrance to a small wadi and hill village. Now the track begins to level out as it follows the wadi bed.

From here and for many kilometres further, the scenery is pure magic and forever changing. There is lush vegetation from beautiful scraggy trees to full green hanging vines. Water sparkling like crystal suddenly appears and at one point trembles over a rock in the fine silver thread of a waterfall. In other places the water meanders slowly through the wadi, often forming wide pools, teeming with toads and "instant fish".

Sometimes there is a track to follow, which may suddenly lead one steeply upwards to circuit a narrow rock-strewn gorge and then down again through the water; or it may unexpectedly disappear among an unruly tide of boulders scattered over the wadi bed by past floods. There are small patches of soft sand to negotiate, surprise drops in level to shock the unwary and sharp slides of stones, reducing speed to a snail's pace. In short, there is almost every type of terrain to test the driver's skills.

The bird life cannot fail to catch the attention even of those least interested in birds. Dark brown hammerkops, wading in the water like their prehistoric ancestors and said in parts of Africa to bring good luck, soon become a common sight, as do egrets and herons. Sand partridges, sunbirds, bee-eaters, blackbush robins and weaverbirds, with their enchanting colonies of nests swinging from trees, streak between the bushes or hop and run over the rocks.

During one short stop, I spotted a handsome long blue lizard lazing in the sun on a smooth round boulder *(see inset)*. Then he disappeared in a flash of blue, leaving me doubting his very existence, gone in an instant like a rainbow.

Along the wadi are occasional small farms, apparently supported by little more than a flock of goats, sometimes a few camels and bees in bright low beehives. A few farms have donkeys and some have sheep. The farm houses are small, simple, square blocks, many transformed by their owners into works of art, with colourful, geometric designs painted on their walls, as if inspired by the beauty of the valley.

The inhabitants of the wadi gaze in wonder at the madmen who bump past in their vehicles. The women, often in brightly coloured dresses, turn shyly away and the odd huntsman with his gun over his shoulder, leading a loaded camel home, or a man, with flowers in his hair, caught at his ablutions in the river, questions why we are blundering through their territory.

As the day progresses the magic begins to fade. At each twist in the wadi, one believes this is where the mountains will end and the desert begin, but at each turn there is another line of mountains stretching far away in front. Gradually the land becomes more arid, until finally you are bowling along over seemingly endless small hills of sand and rock. Then finally there are signs of denser population, houses, a big school, a mosque and suddenly a tarmac road. The road leads to al Lith and, from there, it is a straight run home beside the sea to the Makkah road and so back to Jeddah.

DIRECTIONS

Take the expressway to Makkah. SET YOUR ODOMETER AT **0** by the green palm sculpture, at the junction of al Falah Street and the expressway.

Drive towards Taif via the non-Muslim by-pass around Makkah.

To by-pass Taif, at odometer reading 162 km turn off at an EXIT sign and a sign for the Massarah Intercontinental Hotel onto the Riyadh ring road.

Drive on until you reach a flyover at odometer reading about 169 km. Turn right under the flyover onto a slip road and the main road towards Taif centre again. After 1 km turn left at the lights onto King Khalid Road.

Follow this ring road round until you get to a T-junction and traffic lights at odometer reading 180 km and turn left. There is a police checkpoint almost immediately. You are now on the Abha road.

About 7 km further on is a petrol station, where it is wise to fill up. Soon after this is a sign to al Bahah and a sign reading "Abha 554 km".

Drive 10 km past the petrol station and turn right at the sign to Bani Saad, odometer reading 190.8 km

Bani Saad is approximately 46 km down this road. Continue through Bani Saad, then through Kaladaa, which is 51.6 km from the turn-off. Pass a turn to Lughab to the left. A few kilometres further, 17 km from Bani Saad, as the road bends to the left, immediately after a crash barrier on the right and at the top of a rise, is a track on the right.

Turn onto the track, which almost doubles back and then twists round to the left again and down the mountain side, leading to a good campsite on a flattish platform just off to the right of the track, which continues steeply down the escarpment.

The wadi from Bani Saad campsite

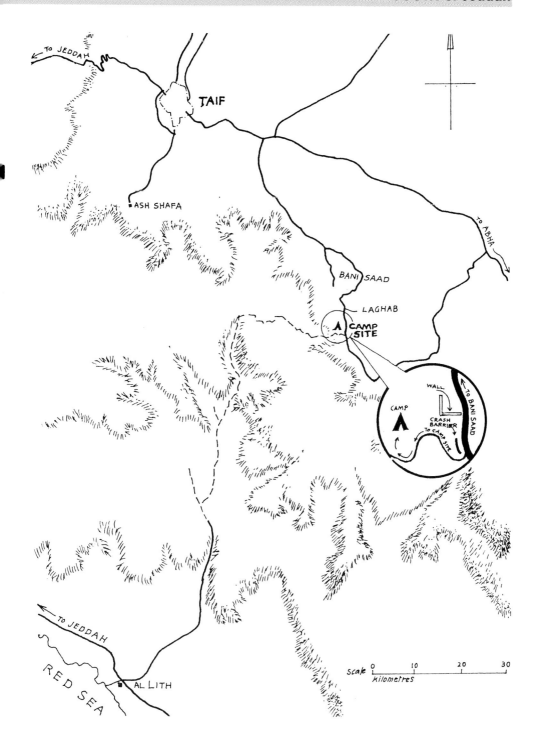

TO JEDDAH

TAIF

ASH SHAFA

TO ABHA

BANI SAAD

LAGHAB

CAMP SITE

WALL

TO BANI SAAD

CAMP

CRASH BARRIER

TO CAMP SITE

TO JEDDAH

RED SEA

AL LITH

Scale

0   10   20   30

kilometres

51

18 Wadi Milh

DAY OR WEEKEND TRIP (1½ hrs)

4 WHEEL DRIVE

Wadi Milh, below the foothills of the Sarawat mountains, is an ideal place to go for a quiet picnic to get away from Jeddah for a day and equally good for a relaxing night's camping without too much driving. It is barely an hour's drive out of Jeddah approaching the foothills of the Sarawat mountains.

The wadi meanders between rocky crags, narrow and stony with patches of sand and scattered with low acacias. It is attractive and peaceful with no sound to be heard but the calls of birds, of which there are plenty, and the occasional pick-up vehicle bumping along the track, heading higher into the wadi.

It is too wild for cultivation, in spite of its proximity to the fertile Wadi Fatima with its gushing water wells. In Wadi Milh we passed two more primitive wells, where the water is wound up by hand in a bucket. One was dry, but the other had water and was evidently very much in use. As we stood peering into the depths, some local men rode up - in their pick-ups, I have to say, rather than on camels, though I half expected them to be wild tribesmen come to establish ownership of their water and to chase off the "alien tribe". Instead they were extremely friendly, although at first somewhat puzzled as to why these foreigners should want to roam their valleys, and then highly amused to find we took pleasure in watching their birds, which they told us were nothing more than a good meal for them.

We had seen what we thought were long-legged buzzards; they told us they were eagles and identified them in our book as booted eagles. Besides these we saw black bush robins, wheatears, shrikes and numerous enchanting little bee-eaters.

There are several good places to camp. Our choice was perhaps a little too close to the track. However we were disturbed only briefly in the night by some inquisitive passing travellers. In the morning we saw one young bedu running barefoot over sharp flints and jagged rocks on feet of leather.

The night was still with that deep silence you forget exists in the low murmuring hum of the city at night. The sky was a glittering mass of stars crossed by an occasional bat flitting low.

In the spring or after the rains this must be an idyllic wadi to visit.

The well at Wadi Milh

DIRECTIONS

There are two possible routes to Wadi Milh, one, the shorter and more direct, takes you through Bahrah to Jamoum; and the other, approximately 20 km further, but quieter, runs via Usfan and then south to Jamoum.

For the Bahrah route, leave Jeddah on the Makkah expressway. SET YOUR ODOMETER AT **0** by the palm sculpture at the junction with al Falah St.

At 16 km turn left, following the sign to Bahrah. After about 1 km turn right at the traffic lights and on through Bahrah, following the road to Jamoum.

Go through Jamoum and over the Medina/Makkah road at 59.2 km.

Continue for a further 16 km and at 75.2 km, turn left onto a little road, signed Qushashiah. SET YOUR ODOMETER AT **0**.

You are now driving up a wide wadi, Wadi Fatima, and will see a large and seemingly new dam 2.5 km ahead of you. Drive towards the dam and when you reach it, take the track to the right, which leads you up and around it.

At the highest point as you circuit the dam, you will see Wadi Fatima, wide and sandy-bedded stretching in front of you and bearing slightly to the right. Far over to the left, behind a spur of rock, runs another wadi, at first almost parallel to Fatima. This is Wadi Milh. You can reach it either by crossing Wadi Fatima and rounding the spur or by driving up Wadi Fatima for about 3.5 km.

Here, at 6.2 km, on the left-hand rocky side of the wadi, a steep track climbs excitingly and descends into Wadi Milh only 2.4 km away. In the wadi turn right and drive up until you find a campsite you like.

If you live in north Jeddah, a longer route, but in our opinion more agreeable with less traffic, goes via Usfan.

Turn off the ring road expressway going north to Usfan. SET YOUR ODOMETER AT **0**. At 26.5 km just after passing a Turkish fort on your left, just before Usfan, turn right to Makkah at Exit 34. Follow this road until Exit 38 and turn left onto Taif road at odometer 80 km.

After a further 16 km, turn off left to Qushashiah and continue as directed above.

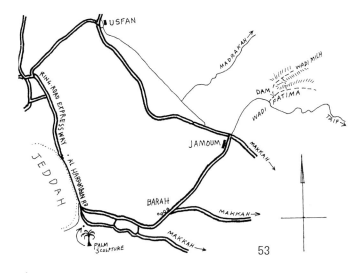

53

19 **Wadi Rhyasan**

DAY OR WEEKEND TRIP (1½ hrs)

2WHEEL DRIVE **4**WHEEL DRIVE

(campsite 2)

Wadi Rhyasan, known by many as Wadi Kara, lies in the foothills of the Taif escarpment. Beautiful and spectacular formations of rock rise up within and beside the wadi. It is an easy and pleasant drive from Jeddah.

It appears to have thriving farming communities at intervals down the wadi, with a scattering of small houses and fitfully throbbing generators driving the pumps, irrigating the plots.

The tracks lead over man-made embankments of sand, criss-crossing the wadi here and there to control irrigation and for protection against flash floods.

Wadi Rhyasan

There are many good places to camp in this attractive wadi. Of the two mentioned here, the first is up a side wadi, which comes to a dead end in about 2 to 3 km, and the other is in a left-hand branch of the main wadi, approximately 10 km further on.

The first, almost entirely enclosed by mountains, has large areas of soft sand and it would therefore be unwise to attempt the last part without a 4-wheel drive. The wadi ends in a large sandy circle, with patches of thorny bushes. On one side there may be a herd of goats penned in for the night with their keepers sleeping near-by, but the area is large enough, with enough bushes and rocks to accommodate everyone with space and privacy. The only sad and serious disadvantage of this lovely site is that there is a lot of litter that not even the goats will chew up. However, it is still possible to find litter-free areas, especially if you push through the bushes at the base of the mountain.

There is a good pre-breakfast climb up any of the peaks, with a fine view of surrounding mountains and wadis from the top. Coming down can be hazardous in places, in particular where a cleft in the rock drops sheer down into a deep and sinister stagnant pool.

For the sharp-eyed - if less energetic - a stroll over the gravelly sand near the rocks may be rewarding. Here little pieces of amazonite, a turquoise-coloured mineral sometimes used as a semi-precious stone, can be found.

The second campsite we chose further into the main wadi is on a raised platform of shingly ground, dotted with acacias. Lying slightly below and to one side are large, flat, pitted and interestingly eroded rocks. There is an impressive view back down the wadi and the hills on the east provide shade from the early sun.

On our first visit to this site, we had three children with us between the ages of one and five and they entertained themselves happily, scrambling over the rocks and adventuring off to find flocks of goats and baby camels.

At both sites one may see all sorts of small birds, as well as doves, kestrels, ravens, Egyptian vultures and owls, which may wake you with their nocturnal screeches.

DIRECTIONS

Take the Makkah road. SET YOUR ODOMETER AT **0** by the palm sculpture at the junction of al Falah Street, from Jeddah Islamic Sea Port and al Haramain road, the expressway.

Head for Taif, taking the non-Muslim by-pass around Makkah. After rejoining the main Makkah-Taif road, drive for less than 1 km to a petrol station on the right (ODOMETER READING 103).

Approximately 0.5 km further, turn sharp right off the road between the fencing at a sign, which reads "AL RASHID ABETONG SWEDE-BEAM SYSTEM ". RE-SET YOUR ODOMETER AT **0**. Go on for 100 yards towards ARASS and then take the track bearing left, heading south-east, leaving it on your right. Continue S.E. for about 1 km and then bear right a little to enter a wide wadi. There is a chicken factory at the entrance about 1 km to your left, as you turn in. Drive on another 1.5 km and you will reach a date palm grove on your left. Continue past the date palms, keeping to the left side of the wadi, and a few kilometres further, take the track leading left into the side wadi, which brings you to the first campsite at odometer reading 8.5 km.

For the second campsite, pass this side wadi and after a few hundred yards you will see a school house on the left, followed by a cluster of houses and a handsome white mosque on your right. SET YOUR ODOMETER AT **0**.

Continue for about 1 km and then branch left, passing around a small hill of rocks on your right. Ahead you will see two pinnacle rocks. The one on the right is a twisted, screw shape. Drive between them and as you pass the twisted pinnacle, your odometer should read 4.5 km. Now keep to the right side and at 7.8 km is another small hamlet and a tiny white mosque on your right. You are now 1 km from the campsite. Continue on the track for 0.6 km, and turn left in a hairpin, crossing the wadi about 100 yards from the base of the escarpment. The ground rises sharply onto a natural platform with a scattering of low acacias and a plentiful supply of dead wood. Looking back you will see a huge rock like the Rock of Gibraltar at exactly 340°. Here is the second campsite.

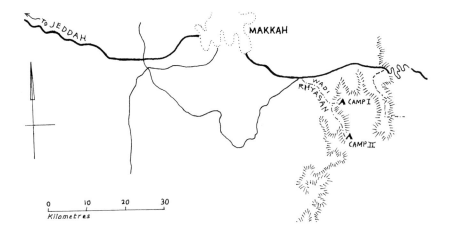

20 The Camel Trail

DAY OR WEEKEND TRIP (2 hrs)

4 WHEEL DRIVE

This expedition should appeal to those who like to search and discover something for themselves and also to those who enjoy a trek in the mountains, but don't necessarily feel driven by the relentless urge to find something of significance.

If you have already walked among the peaks of the escarpment at Harithi *(see trek to Harithi)*, you may have found the head of the old camel trail, where it reaches the summit in a final sweep on the long ascent from the valley far below. You may want to see more of it and find where it levels out at the foot of the mountains en route to Makkah or Jeddah. The obvious answer would be to try and follow the path down. However it could take up to 4 hours to reach the wadi. Would you then have the stamina to climb up again or is there a distinctive landmark to make a rendezvous with a lower based party? Finding the base first might be wiser.

It was with this in mind that we set off early one Friday morning and drove up the wadi that runs north-west/south-east at the bottom of the escarpment below al Hadr. The wadi is wide to start with, with small pockets of habitation on the higher ground and well banked-up fields of cultivation. There is a tangle of tracks running in all directions, but it is not too difficult to find your way up the wadi. However, it becomes increasingly hard to drive, as the wadi bed changes and is finally strewn with stones and boulders. A track of sorts can be found nonetheless.

On the left, the mountains rear up, peak after peak, ending in a jagged skyline several thousand feet above. If you are familiar with the edge of the escarpment at Harithi, you will recognise the steep pointed pinnacles of rock. To the right of them, looking upwards, is a shallower gap between the peaks. This is where the camel trail winds up and over the top.

Exactly where the trail begins or ends in the wadi, we are still uncertain. We know you must drive up about 15 km and then begin the search behind each promontory of rock for evidence of man-made paths, leading up gentle inclines. It may be that flash floods have swept away all trace of them so low in the foothills.

Armed with a good supply of water, we finally began a climb up towards our goal by way of the mouth of a relatively wide side wadi. As we gained the lower peaks, we hoped that suddenly all would be revealed and the camel trail would snake down the side or appear round a corner. Although the very top of the trail became clearer, we did not go high enough to find any further evidence. However, with or without a camel trail, it is an extremely pleasant walk, scrambling in the foot-hills of the escarpment. There is shade to be found under big fig trees and comfortable boulders to rest against. The views are stunning and the air grows increasingly clear and fresh.

There are places where it would be pleasant to camp. One in particular lay up a little side wadi that came to a dead end in a small white sandy clearing surrounded by huge smooth boulders. Not far away and lower down this wadi were rows of beehives, some still made of hollowed out tree trunks.

There was some birdlife: sunbirds, bee-eaters, shrikes and weaver birds with their beautifully made nests suspended in the trees. We also saw two beautiful blue and gold agamid lizards. There was evidence, cruelly displayed, that the already rare striped hyenas roam the hills. We saw three that had recently been caught, tied by the back legs and left to die suspended from trees. Striped hyenas live on carrion and dried bones, insects, reptiles and vegetable matter. They will only attack larger mammals if they are starving and are therefore relatively harmless to man and his flocks. A young kid, possibly abandoned by the nanny-goat and who sadly wanted to follow us, would be more threatened by the bands of baboons in the hills than by a hyena. Saudi Arabian protection agencies are putting a stop to the indiscriminate killing of the hyenas.

DIRECTIONS

Leave Jeddah by the Makkah road. SET YOUR ODOMETER AT **0** by the green palm sculpture at the junction of the expressway and al Falah Street. Turn right at 39 km onto the non-Muslim by-pass, rejoining the Makkah/Taif road at about 102 km.

At 122 km turn right off the road immediately before the police checkpoint and a small white mosque. SET YOUR ODOMETER AT **0**. Beside the fence which borders the road you have just left, a tarmac road runs back and branches off immediately to the left. Take this left branch, the surface of which is a smooth packed material. It soon becomes a rough track, bending left and downhill beside another mosque with a green crescent above two green orbs.

At 6 km you pass yet another mosque, with a green crescent above three green orbs. Now head up the wadi, initially keeping to the middle as far as possible, bearing left as you approach 15 km.

Look up to your left to see if you can recognise the top of the camel trail on the sky-line and begin your search for the lower paths.

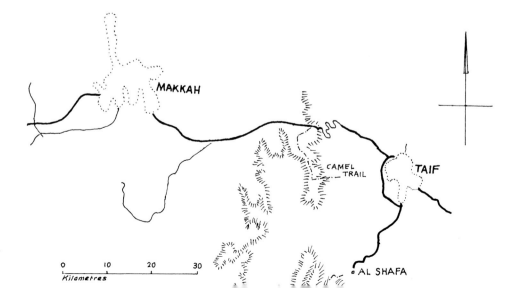

21 Harithl

DAY OR WEEKEND TRIP (2¹/₂-3 hrs)

4 WHEEL
DRIVE

Harithi is a wonderful place to go to escape from the steamy summer heat in Jeddah. It lies in the hills at the brink of the escarpment, 2000 metres high, to the south of al Hada. The air is clear, cool and refreshing and at night you often need warm clothing and extra blankets.

The chosen campsite is on a little terrace, surrounded by rocks, grass, lavender bushes, low juniper and wild fig trees and a variety of flowers and herbs in the rolling, stony hills.

Much of the land around has been cut into terraces, and narrow wadis have been dammed for a scattering of farms growing crops such as beans, tomatoes, cucumbers, pomegranates, apricots, grapes, figs, prickly pears, mulberries, and fields of the highly prized roses, of "Asseer of Roses" (rosewater, scent) fame.

Some old stone buildings have been abandoned and the crude wooden doors still swing open with fine precision, revealing simple and cool interiors. Low stone shelters house hollowed-out tree trunks lying side by side *(see inset)*. These were once beehives, now I suppose replaced by modern and more sophisticated hives, perhaps more productive but certainly less charming.

The walks from the campsite are beautiful. One takes you up between two high pinnacles of rock with a dramatic view of jagged peaks and down the escarpment to the valley thousands of feet below, while above, Egyptian vultures and eagles soar between their eyries in the crags. Another takes you to the top of the camel trail. At first it is hard to recognise it as a camel trail, but if you scramble down a little lower over the stones and tussocks of grass, you will see a wide path of stones laid flat, forming a smooth gentle gradient, descending in slow sweeps to the plain below. It must have been an immense labour creating such a path for the camel trains to pass through the mountains.

This idyllic setting of cool grasses, lavender, roses, juniper, birds, bees, clouds of butterflies around the *acacia mimosa* and numerous other flowers and creatures can, however, show another face of nature, as we once found to our cost. It is the focus of fierce storms, so fierce that no sooner had part of the very rough, stony and steep road been replaced early in 1995 with a tarmac one than it was swept away in a storm, which not only tore up the tarmac but uprooted trees and washed down detritus, obliterating much of the surviving track. We have to admit to getting severely bogged down and stuck in a flood soon after such a storm. A kind and characteristically generous local rosegrower spent three hours of his Thursday evening cheerfully extricating us, without a single grudging word. Grateful to be out of the water and mud, we made camp where we were, only to be woken later in the night by torrential rain, thunder and sheets of dazzling lightning, at which point, fearful of being trapped by further floods, we beat a cautious retreat to safer land out of the mountains.

DIRECTIONS

Leave Jeddah by the Makkah road. SET YOUR ODOMETER AT **0** by the green palm sculpture at the junction of the expressway and al Falah Street.

Drive towards Taif. At the top of the escarpment, your odometer should read 146 km. Fill up with petrol.

At 154.4 km (approximately 6.5 km beyond the Sheraton hotel turning) pass the green-topped Meeqat mosque on your left and another mosque on your right. Turn right almost immediately down a small road, which brings you into what appears to be a builder's yard. Or, to be sure you have the correct one, take the next right turn, 50 yards on, which is signed to Wadi Ghadirain and which also leads into the yard.

In the builder's yard, RE-SET YOUR ODOMETER AT **0**. Turn right and follow the road through the yard. At odometer reading 1 km take the right fork.

At 4.5 km you pass through a small village with a mosque on the right.

At 6.8 km take a sharp right turn uphill. Continue on the track and you will drop down the hill and pass a cluster of houses at 8.5 km. Keep to the left down the hill after the abandoned red water carrier.

At 9.5 km the track forks and there is a sort of triangular island of

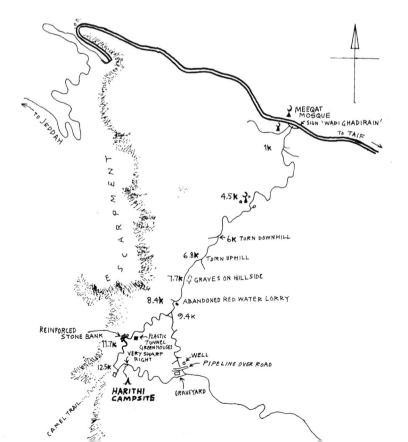

rocks. Unless there has been recent heavy rain, fork right. Keep going up again and down, past a precarious looking reinforced stone bank, up and over another hill and down over a very rough bit of road onto a muddy field at 12.5 km. If this is flooded, do not attempt to cross! Over along the edge of the next field and round to the left and just around the corner of the hill at 13.1 km, there is an extremely sharp and steep turn by some deserted stone houses. The track here climbs very steeply, but just over the top in less than 1 km is a good terrace and campsite.

On your return you may wish to turn right at the bottom of the first little steep run and go back through Harithi village. If so, follow the map carefully.

To find the camel trail, walk north over and round the first rise and, looking down on the rose terraces and farm below, turn westward past a banked-up dam and reservoir towards quite a wide opening between the crags. Here you are on the edge of the escarpment and at the top of the camel trail.

Turning back again, walk until you are almost in sight of the reservoir and dam and then turn to the left and climb a short, but fairly steep, rise between two sharp crags. At the top you are rewarded with a dramatic, awe-inspiring view of sharp pinnacles of rock and steep falls into the valley below.

The Harithi escarpment

22 Turabah Town and the Fossils by Jebel Umm Himar

WEEKEND TRIP (4½ hrs)

4 WHEEL
DRIVE

Khurmah, which lies about 90 km north-east of Turabah, was once an important trading centre on routes from Hejaz to Nejd and to Syria. Khurmah and Turabah were both established towns in the 18th century, perhaps even earlier. The population included two main groups of the Ataibi tribe, whose grazing rights extended into Nejd as well as Hejaz. Part of the population were town dwelling (hadar), who lived by trading, and part were nomadic (bedu), who lived off grazing and looting caravans.

Around 1918 it was an area much coveted by Abdul Aziz Ibn Saud, then ruler of Nejd, and by Hussein, Sharif of Makkah and ruler of Hejaz. However Khalid Ibn Mansur Ibn Luway, Sharif and ruler of Khurmah, refused either to pay taxes to or to be subjugated by Hussein, although he had cooperated with him during the Arab Revolt.

Hussein tried unsuccessfully to capture Khurmah in July, and again in September, 1918. At first Ibn Saud, acting with caution, ignored Khalid's plea for help, but finally in November sent 450 of his men to the area.

There were further minor attacks from Hussein, easily repulsed until Hussein sent his son, Abdullah, with 5000 men, after the Ottoman surrender of Medina.

On the 21st May, 1919, Abdullah conquered Turabah on his way to Khurmah. Ibn Saud then sent a force of 1500 warriors, who joined with Khalid's 4000. Without waiting for Ibn Saud himself, they attacked without delay on the night of the 25th/26th May and crushed Abdullah's force at Turabah, slaughtering 1350 of his men.

Following the battle of Turabah, Ibn Saud had a decisive advantage over Hussein. After fighting further battles in Hejaz and utilising subtle siege tactics, Ibn Saud precipitated the collapse of Hashemite rule. Hussein was exiled, first to Aqaba in 1924, and then to Cyprus the following year.

There is little sign today of that momentous event of less than a century ago. The battle took place around the old part of the town, where you see the remains of the mud houses, surrounded by date palms.

If nothing remains to remind us of the great battle, only about 24 km from Turabah, among the rocks and hills are remnants of the distant past possibly 67 million years ago, when the sea washed over what is now desert. Here, near Jebel Umm Himar, lying scattered on the surface, are many remarkable clusters of fossils. In 1970, a French group found fossils of sharks, turtles, and even crocodiles. It is unlikely you would be quite so lucky as to find anything so exciting, but it is not difficult to come across large clusters of shell fossils and you may find the odd shark's tooth.

There are pleasant places to camp among large smooth rocks and thorn bushes in the desert near Jebel Umm Himar.

DIRECTIONS

Leave Jeddah by the Makkah road. SET YOUR ODOMETER AT **0** by the green palm sculpture at the junction of the expressway and al Falah Street.

Drive towards Taif via the non-Muslim Makkah by-pass. To by-pass Taif, at odometer reading 162 km, turn off at an EXIT sign and a sign for the Massarah Intercontinental Hotel onto the Riyadh ring road.

Drive on until you reach a T junction under a flyover at 169 km. Turn right onto the slip road and the road heading towards Taif centre. After 1.5 km turn left at the lights onto King Khalid Road. Follow this until you get to traffic lights at the T-junction at 180 km and turn left onto the Abha road. There is a checkpoint almost immediately.

RESET YOUR ODOMETER AT **0**. Continue on the Abha road until you reach the sign to Turabah at about 80 km. Take this left turn to Turabah and drive on through the new town, bearing right at an orangey-yellow mosque. At 174 km turn off the road to the right and you will see the remains of the mud houses of old Turabah, some still inhabited, among the palm groves. Here is the site of the famous battle.

FILL UP WITH PETROL. Retrace your way from old Turabah for about 17 km and then turn right into the desert following tracks and drive west-north-west for approximately 13 km. On your right you should see a microwave dish standing high on the slopes of a jebel. Continue westwards for a further 10 km. On the way look out for the more fertile part of the wadi, where there are large smooth rocks and some vegetation. Within the groups of rocks are delightful places to camp.

Slightly to the south-west lies Jebel Umm Himar. All around is barren and desolate stony ground, rising and falling in little hillocks. Scattered on these are the fossils from the shallow sea of 67 million years ago.

It is possible to return via the village of Kulakh, about 60 km over the desert. From Jebel Umm Himar turn north-west and drive approximately 25 km to the track south of Jebel An. Turn west and follow the track to the village of Kulakh, beyond which is a tarmac road, running south-west for about 25 km, where it joins the Abha/Taif road.

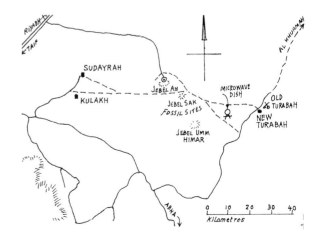

23 The Palace at Old Muwayh

WEEKEND TRIP (5½ hrs)

4 WHEEL DRIVE

This old Turkish fort built towards the end of the last century once garrisoned those who manned the numerous watch towers that can be seen on the hills around the fort. It lies in the desert, a dark grey forbidding ruin, surrounded by the ruins of mud houses, a few of which are still occupied.

Two generations ago King Abdul Aziz refurbished it for his own use, adding a majlis with a long row of marble seats, with his own throne in the centre. According to some of the locals, he came here after he had been to Makkah for Hajj. He used it as a hunting lodge, inviting parties to hunt gazelle and other game, and falconers in pursuit of birds such as partridge and houbara (McQueen's Bustard). Today the gazelle are gone, and smaller game and houbara are rare indeed. A few kilometres away we did see a large dhubb or spiny-tailed lizard, about two feet long, with long legs and inflated belly. It ran surprisingly fast before diving into its burrow.

In King Abdul Aziz's day, an airstrip was cleared for his Dakota to land.

Opposite the main entrance to the fort is a large flat area of sabkhah - crusted salt-marsh. It floods after a rainfall, leaving a salt deposit that forms a fragile crust, treacherous for vehicles when it's wet beneath.

To the north and north-east in a gully among the rocks and low hills are numerous wells, still used by water lorries and by the local people for their flocks. At times the water table rises to within a foot of the surface. Here are a few low shrubs. There are some quite pleasant places to camp amongst the low hills nearby.

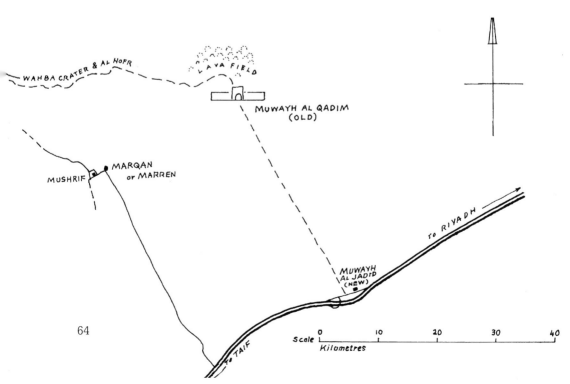

64

DIRECTIONS

The distance is about 420 km from Jeddah and takes about 5 hours including stops.

Leave Jeddah by the Makkah road. SET YOUR ODOMETER AT **0** by the green palm sculpture, at the junction of the expressway and al Falah Street.

Drive towards Taif. On the outskirts, at odometer reading 162 km, go under a flyover and turn right immediately, following the sign to Riyadh. At the turn is a sign for the Massarah Intercontinental Hotel. Follow the by-pass for about 6 km until you are at a T junction under a flyover. Turn left onto the Riyadh road.

RE-SET ODOMETER AT **0**. Continue for 170 km past Radwan to New Muwayh. Fill up with petrol at Radwan or New Muwayh. Turn off the main road at the signpost to Muwayh and go across the main road via the flyover. Take the right turn at the T junction leading into New Muwayh and almost immediately swing left into the sand (just before you get into the village). RE-SET YOUR ODOMETER AT **0**. Now head north-north-west 335° for 40 km. On the horizon you will soon see a low line of hills and a square watchtower gradually becomes discernible. Then you will see the lighter coloured, mud minaret of Old Muwayh village mosque and finally the long line of the ruined palace nearby.

The palace at Old Muwayh

24 The Wahba Crater

WEEKEND TRIP (5½ hrs)

4 WHEEL DRIVE

The Wahba crater, the largest of its kind in western Arabia, is a spectacular and impressive sight. Approaching from just west of south, bumping over the sandy plain, with no hint of any crater within miles, the ground rises ahead of you, and reaching the top, you must turn sharply or plummet into the heart of the crater, a heartstopping moment. The rising ground is the encircling lip of the crater and no harmless hillock as it first appeared.

The crater is 2 km wide and the cliffs drop steeply 260 metres to a flat base, in the centre of which is a huge salt pan, half a kilometre across, where there was once a lake. The cliffs are broken on the north-east edge by a few more gentle gorges and slightly further north is the surprising sight of a verdant shelf or terrace about two-thirds of the way up. Here grow tall palm trees and long, luscious, green grass, an extraordinary surprise in such a harsh landscape.

There has been much speculation as to the origin of the crater. One theory is that it was caused by the impact of a meteorite. Geologists now think that a volcanic eruption was the cause. It lies in an area where there was intense volcanic activity in the past. The surrounding "sandy" plain is in fact a bed of volcanic ash. To the north-west is a mound with a vertical face on the edge of the crater, which was an earlier volcano, split in half when the crater was formed. In this cliff face can be seen lava-filled dykes.

The vast eruption that must have occurred apparently could have been caused by water seeping down into the underground chambers of hot molten rock, causing a huge subterranean explosion. The cooling and contracting thereafter left this immense hole.

It is possible to climb down one of the side gorges on the north perimeter of the crater, the one on which the palm garden grows being the gentlest. It takes about 40 minutes to get down, so it is advisable to go early while the shadows are still long in the bowl of the crater and to take a good supply of water. Then when you come up again, you can afford the time and luxury of lying in the long, wet grass at the feet of the palm trees;

but watch out for snakes. This fertile terrace is fed by springs seeping out of the cliff face. The water, which has run through the porous volcanic layers, meets the pre-Cambrian solid basement rock at this level and here finds an outlet in the crater walls.

On the higher ledges around the top of the crater there are good places to camp with a spectacular view! Or if you prefer, there are some perfect secluded places among the hollows and bays of the "young lava", which has run in shallow ripples over the ground to the north and east of the crater.

Around a peninsula of the "young lava" to the north, about 20 km north-north-east of the crater, is a lake, roughly 3 km long, surrounded by low trees and acacias. The waters are muddy and probably rife with bilharzia, but it is a tranquil and pleasant sight.

The Wahba crater

DIRECTIONS

Leave Jeddah by the Makkah road. SET YOUR ODOMETER AT **0** by the palm sculpture at the junction of the expressway and al Falah Sreet.

Drive towards Taif. On the outskirts at odometer reading 162 km go under a flyover and turn right immediately onto the by-pass to Riyadh. At the turn is a sign for the Massarah Intercontinental Hotel. Follow the bypass for about 6 km until you are at a T-junction under a flyover. Turn left onto the Riyadh road.

Continue on the Riyadh road, pass the turn to Radwan at odometer reading 292 km, and 43 km further, at 335 km, turn left at the sign to Marren or Marqan. RE-SET YOUR ODOMETER AT **0**.

At odometer reading 44 km turn left at a T-junction to Mushrif. In the village of Mushrif at 47 km turn right. At 48 km turn left. Continue north-west.

Soon the road becomes a graded track. (They are extending the road.)

At 80 km you should have reached al Hofr, an area of villages and cultivation, which is not marked on any map but is well known in the area. There is an old cara-vanserai and fort on a bleak rocky mound.

Here, in one of the villages, you will find petrol.

About 6.5 km north of al Hofr is the crater. A huge ash cone, hollowed out by the crater, and a horse-shoe volcano on its west side are visible from near the village, giving you an indication of the crater, which is invisible until you are upon it.

There is an alternative way for the more adventurous. Turn off the Riyadh road at the turn to Radwan. You will see a radio tower on the north-west side of the road. At a starting position east of the radio tower RE-SET YOUR ODOMETER AT **0**. Take a 345° bearing and drive approximately 90 km across the desert to al Hofr.

The palm garden.

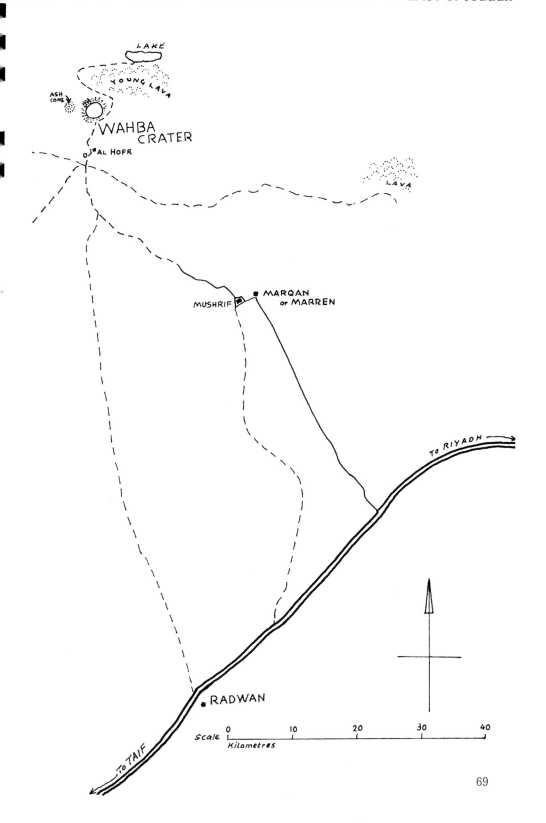

25 **Pools on Darb Zubaida**

WEEKEND TRIP (3½ hrs)

4 WHEEL
DRIVE

The ancient road, known as the Darb Zubaida, runs from Kufa, south of Baghdad, to Makkah. Although parts of it may have been in use in pre-Islamic times, it was the Abbasid Caliphs and contemporary wealthy philanthropists who firmly established the road and provided facilities for the huge caravans of pilgrims travelling to Makkah. The best known of these benefactors is Queen Zubaida, from whom the road took its name.

Zubaida was the favourite wife of the fifth Abbasid Caliph, Harun ar-Rashid (786-809 AD), who was reputed to have presided over a sumptuous court at Baghdad. The world knows of him from "The Arabian Nights".

Zubaida was renowned for her piety and her generosity, in particular for the time and money she spent on the welfare of the pilgrims. At her instigation, wells were dug and water cisterns and shelters built, as well as hospitals, palaces, forts and caravanserais. These served the many pilgrims travelling the road with hundreds of camels or simply on foot.

Her most remarkable achievement was the aqueduct, Ain Zubaida, that she constructed to provide sufficient water for the Holy City of Makkah. Also of prime importance are the large watering holes or reservoirs, fed by water col-lected in canals, or qanats. Here at the southern end of the Darb Zubaida, the water runs across the plateau from the Sarawat mountains, where the rainfall is plentiful.

Two of the most impressive and accessible watering holes, or birqats, can be found on the Darb Zubaida north-east of Taif. These are the Birqat al Aqiq and the Birqat al Khuraba. They were cleared and renovated in 1973 and similar square birqats were built in concrete nearby. The local bedouin still use the water they supply.

Birqat al Aqiq, sometimes called simply al Birqah, is 112 km north-east of Taif, on the eastern edge of Wadi al Aqiq. It is located a few hundred metres west of the road running north from Ashayrah to Mohani. The denser, shady trees around it make it possible to identify it from the road.

This pool is square, each side measuring 49 metres at the top. The sides are stepped and the depth is said to be 5 metres. Around the top runs a protective wall, broken by doorways for access. The water channel runs in at the south-west corner.

Nearby are the ruins and outlines of the old settlement buildings and cara-vanserais. It is thought there was a square fort here, with round towers at each corner. Both these and the pool are made of volcanic stones.

The explorer Richard Burton, who referred briefly to Birqat al Aqiq, rem-arked that all these cisterns were surrounded by different types of trees. We were told that the best time to visit is in the spring, since that is when the trees are in blossom.

Birqat al Khuraba lies in the desert on the other side of the road, about 14 km south-east. This water place has great charm. It is a double pool linked by a

Birqat al Khuraba

little two-domed arched building, which straddles two tunnels connecting the pools. The first, to the west, is rectangular, with stepped sides measuring about 36 x 28 metres. This is the catchment or settling tank from which the water flows when it has risen high enough, through the tunnels into the larger pool. This larger pool is beautifully circular and stepped from top to bottom. It is about 40 metres in diameter.

Water used to flow in through a qanat running from Wadi Aqiq, about 25 km away. Within easy distance are several other birqats to the north. The nearest, about 16 km away, is Birqat al Ghazlaniyyah, which is a round pool, almost completely filled in and about 28 metres in diameter. It is low lying and is surrounded by trees and vegetation, which makes it a picturesque picnic place. There seems to be at least one small well that is now silted up.

About 14 km north again is al Mislah, which we have not been to, but are told is a beautifully-built pool. There are buttresses at each corner, external semi-circular buttresses on the north and east walls and rectangular buttresses on the west wall. It is divided, part of the southern side forming a clearing pool, and is built in the middle of the wadi. Unfortunately, it too has almost completely filled up with sand.

With time you can go further to Khabra al Haj, Dlay ash Shaqq and so on all the way to Kufa and Baghdad!

To the south, in the foothills of the Sarawat mountains, lie the remains of the last birqat before Makkah. This I have described in the trek in search of the last birqats.

After the fall of Baghdad to the Mongols in the mid-thirteenth century, the Darb Zubaida became unsafe to travel. It was therefore neglected and many of the way-stations fell into disrepair, so it is pleasing that some of the pools have been restored and interesting to see that new ones have been built. The ancient methods of water collection clearly cannot be improved on.

Camping is pleasant by either of the first pools. Birqat al Khuraba is further from the tarmac road and therefore possibly quieter, but you can see some bedouin or farmers moving across the desert and distant lights in the night.

DIRECTIONS

Leave Jeddah by the Makkah road. SET YOUR ODOMETER AT **0** by the green palm sculpture, at the junction of the expressway and al Falah Street.

By-pass Makkah to the south and drive up the escarpment towards Taif. On the outskirts, at about 162 km, there is a sign to Riyadh and the road goes under a flyover. Turn right, following the sign to Riyadh. At the turn is a green sign for the Massarah Intercontinental Hotel.

Follow the by-pass for about 7 km, ignoring the sign for Riyadh at 6 km, until you are at a T junction under a flyover. Turn left onto the Riyadh road. At this junction there is no sign for Riyadh.

RE-SET YOUR ODOMETER AT **0**. Continue on the Riyadh road. At 32 km on your right are the ruins of an old Turkish fort, and then the Arafah garage. At 41.5 km turn off to Ashayrah at Exit 54.

Follow the road through Ashayrah and continue north for approximately another 50 km. At 112.5 km, on your left, in the midst of a group of taller trees about 300 metres from the road, is Birqat al Aqiq.

To find Birqat al Khuraba, return to the road and turn south again. Drive for about 4 km to a point where the road goes between two concrete banks running east-west. Just before it, on the east side of the road, are two signs to al Adil and to al Adil School, both facing south. Turn between them and drive east, following the bank and channel for about 12 km. It leads you directly to Birqat al Khuraba.

To see Zubaida's final pool before Makkah, take the following directions on your return to Jeddah. At Exit 54, as you rejoin the Riyadh/Taif road, RE-SET YOUR ODOMETER AT **0**.

After 24 km, turn right to Makkah and Sayl al Kaybir. At 28.5 km, turn right again to Makkah, Jeddah and Makir al Sail. At 85 km, turn right to Jeddah (left is the "Muslim only" road to Makkah). Drive for about 5 km, just past a turn to al Madiq Hazm. In less than 0.5 km turn off the road to the right at the end of a crash barrier. Double round to the right behind a rocky outcrop, following the track between small white marker posts. There, tucked against the rocks on your right, you will see the final pool.

To return to Jeddah, go back to the road and continue the way you were going, following the road, which passes through Jamjoum, and finally leads to Jeddah.

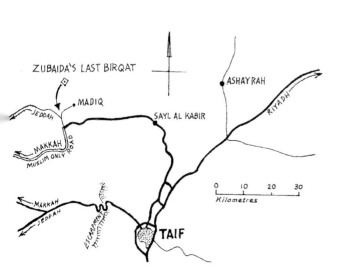

26 **In Search of the Last Birqats**

WEEKEND TRIP (4 hrs)

4 WHEEL
DRIVE

Some trips do not go entirely as planned and many have unforeseen surprises. The anticipation of the unexpected adds to the excitement and enjoyment of trekking. Even if we fail to achieve an objective, there has never been a trip we have regretted or one where we have gained nothing. This particular trek might be deemed a failure, since we found no more of Zubaida's birqats, but it is worth including both for the enjoyable journey, and as the link between the last ruined birqat before Makkah and the well-restored birqats of Aqiq and Khuraba.

Queen Zubaida *(see trek to The Pools on Darb Zubaida)*, who paid much attention to the welfare of the Muslim pilgrims, gave orders that each birqat, or watering hole, should be no further apart than one day's march, probably about 20 to 30 km. We travelled the pilgrimage route in reverse, starting at the Madiq birqat, the last birqat before Makkah, as far as we know. From here to Birqat al Aqiq is between 90 to 100 km, we estimate. Therefore, even allowing for natural watering holes formed by springs, there should once have been perhaps three or even four more birqats or way-stations.

The birqat at al Madiq has been sadly neglected, but the ruins show it was about 15 to 20 metres square, three or four metres deep, with semi-circular buttresses on the inside and a narrow flight of stairs leading down to where the water would have been. Nearby, there are the broken remains of water channels that once fed it and signs of an old well.

Taking the birqat at al Madiq as the starting point, drive up a tarmac road a few kilometres to al Madiq, which looks as if it was once an attractive village, built at different levels at the head of a gorge. Some of the houses on the higher level have a magnificent view through the mountains towards Makkah and some, now abandoned, look as if they were once impressive, with a more affluent style of architecture than the average village houses.

Beyond al Madiq, there is a track which leads up the sandy wadi between high steep mountains. Looking at the sheer cliffs of sand formed at frequent intervals, one can imagine the torrent of water that could race down this gorge after a heavy rainfall.

On either side, on raised ground, are occasional oases with palm groves, the palms sometimes dwarfed by plantations of tall papaya. Somewhere here in this fertile ground, perhaps, lie the remains of an ancient birqat. Although we detoured from the track a few times, we did not wish to be invasive. A few local men we asked appeared never to have heard of Zubaida, her birqats or even the Darb. In their opinion a sensible pilgrim would journey from distant places by aeroplane - we must be mad to think that anyone would walk to Makkah from Baghdad!

Along the path we met a long train of at least fifty fine camels. At the tail end, a little new-born was bleating for its mother, who, walking just ahead, peered round from time to time to make sure he was following. A distance behind, trotting on their camels, rode the two herdsmen.

The mountain sides of the wadi are steep and seldom broken by side wadis into which one might venture to find secluded camping sites. Where there are side wadis, there are little pockets of habitation. So we pressed on in the fading light, through a village where the wadi divides, and turned northwards, following the Darb Zubaida into less precipitous terrain.

Still there are scattered farms and habitation. But turn eastward on a track leading to Ashayrah and here is what looks like ideal camping country. However, all is not what is seems. Twice, a few kilometres up this track, we turned off into a little backwater, only to be scouted out almost at once by firm, but not unfriendly, local men, telling us that this was not a good place to stay. A few kilometres further would be acceptable, but not here. We drove on another 8 km and in the moonless dark, left the track and drove behind the solid shadow of a tall rocky outcrop. Fortuitously, it turned out to be an ideal place. We were left undisturbed and woke in the morning to a beautiful sunrise over the rocky hill, which provided shade as well as protection from curious eyes. There was the sandy bed of a shallow, winding side wadi beside us and little sunbirds in an acacia nearby.

It was suggested later that we had tried to stop in an area sacred to the pilgrims, perhaps where they had once begun the prayers and preparations before their arrival at the Holy City of Makkah. Small wonder that, as infidels, we were not welcome.

Our campsite is marked on the map, but I suggest you leave Jeddah no later than 12.30 pm to find it in the daylight, allowing for stops on the way.

To continue along the Darb Zubaida, retrace your way back along the Ashayrah track until you reach the fork and continue in a north-easterly direction. Once out of the mountains and up on the plateau, the terrain changes to a bleaker, more austere landscape. One pities the poor pilgrims who struggled across this before they reached a more sheltered haven.

Here the tracks run in all directions, but if you follow those that take you north-east, with luck you will find yourselves on the one that brings you onto the tarmac road near the Birqat al Aqiq. Or if, like us, you bear too far east, you meet the same road further south. I don't think there is any danger in missing this road entirely as it runs north a long way. But be sure you have enough petrol before you leave al Madiq.

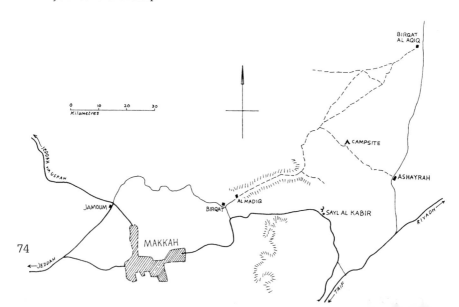

74

DIRECTIONS

Starting from north Jeddah, we chose an alternative route to the normal one, which is a little longer, but avoids a lot of traffic. Take the road north from Jeddah to Usfan. SET YOUR ODOMETER AT **0** at the junction of the ring road expressway, al Haramain Road and the Usfan Road. At 5 km on the Usfan Road is a police checkpoint. At 27 km at Exit 34 turn onto the road to Makkah. Follow this road towards Makkah until, at 80.5 km on the outskirts of Jamoum, turn left onto the road to Taif. At 136.6 km on the left of the road, you will see a lot of small white marker posts. Turn left off the road here and follow a track, to the ruins of the last birqat.

SET YOUR ODOMETER AT **0**. Continue on the track to the Madiq road.. Turn left to al Madiq at 6 km and bear right, into the wadi. Drive up the wadi until at around 31 km you reach a village. Leave the village to your right on the left-hand track, which turns due north.

Follow the track and, at about 45 km, there is a fork with a small metal sign written in Arabic. The left-hand fork should be the continuation of the Darb Zubaida. We forked right here to look for a camping site. The track soon becomes a well-beaten one, leading on to Ashayrah. We turned off it to the left after about 11 km and camped behind a rocky outcrop, approximately 0.5 km from the track, odometer reading 56.5. Before leaving camp, SET YOUR ODOMETER AT **0**. Return to the fork and bend sharply to the right, into the left-hand track of the fork.

At 12.8 km, the track forks again. Turn right and proceed in a north-easterly direction. At a T junction, at about 23.5 km, turn left towards a small village. In the village, bear right again, following tracks in a north-easterly direction, until you meet the road running north from Ashayrah to al Faysiliyah. Continue to Birqat al Aqiq at about 80 km.

To return to Jeddah by road from Birqat al Aqiq, get onto the road and SET YOUR ODOMETER AT **0**. Drive south to Ashayrah, odometer reading 49 km. Continue through Ashayrah to the Riyadh road at 71 km. Turn right towards Taif.

At about 93 km, turn off to the right following the signs to Makkah and Sayl al Kabir. After 5 km, at odometer reading 98 km, turn right again to Megat al Sayl, Makkah and Jeddah. Drive through Sayl al Kabir and, at 151.1 km, turn right at the exit to Jeddah.

The last birqat, al Madiq

27 Camel Races and Ukaz Suq

DAY OR WEEKEND TRIP (3 hrs)

2 WHEEL DRIVE **4** WHEEL DRIVE

There is an area of desert north-east of Taif, not far off the Riyadh road, where you will see a number of camps surrounded by herds of lean camels. These are the racing camels, who come from all over the Gulf to train and run here. The highlights of the year are the annual races held on alternate Thursdays throughout August and early September.

A few years ago the races, although no less serious, had a pleasantly chaotic and rather amateur appearance. They were run in a straight line between high banks of sand to discourage the camels from running out. Then the course was made into a 10 km circuit with parallel sand-banks, except at the beginning and end, where smart post-and-rail fences were constructed. This often had a confusing effect on the camels, who, aware of the obstructing sand-banks, would make few attempts to run off course, until the sand-banks ended and the railings began. The more recalcitrant would decide that at last an escape route had opened up, and so would head for the rails. Finding they were thwarted, they would turn and run in the opposite direction.

Now the course looks thoroughly professional with railings around the entire circumference, a Royal or VIP enclosure, and the diminutive jockeys bedecked in brightly coloured "silks" of a sort. Some of them have earphones and radios to receive instructions, one presumes, from the camel owners or trainers, who roar around the course in vehicles accompanying the race in a cloud of sand, flashing lights and blowing horns.

Even the start has become slicker and not quite the pandemonium it used to be. Now only the camels about to race, plus their "starters", are driven up to the starting rope, where they jostle together in a tumultuous crowd. As the rope drops, the "starters", who are older, stronger and more experienced boys, riding camels alongside the racers, beat the racing camels into action, running their own camels beside them for the first few hundred metres of wild confusion, before dropping back and out of the race.

The races start at about 3 pm and the last one is run at about 6 pm. Then there is just time to find the remains of the Ukaz Suq, and perhaps watch the sun go down behind it.

The Ukaz Suq was once the largest and best known of the pre-Islamic gathering places for commercial, political and social purposes and as a forum for prose and poetry recitation. Now little more than the outlines of the walls of the pre-Islamic buildings remain, but of later additions some walls and an arched doorway still stand. The suq was still used in the 8th century AD, but was attacked and pillaged by a hostile sectarian group towards the end of the century.

A fence has recently been erected around the site to protect it, one supposes, no longer from marauding tribes, but from inquisitive, straying camels or their acquisitive guardians.

You can take the alternative route back to Jeddah, north of Makkah via Sayl al Kaybir. A pleasant change, this descends more gently onto the Tihama plain.

The arched doorway at Ukaz Suq
The Camel Races

DIRECTIONS

Leave Jeddah by the Makkah road. SET ODOMETER AT **0** by the green palm sculpture, at the junction of al Falah Street and the expressway.

By-pass Makkah to the south and drive up the escarpment towards Taif. On the outskirts at about 162 km, there is a sign to Riyadh, and the road goes under a flyover. Turn right, following the sign to Riyadh. At the turn is a green sign to the Massarah Intercontinental Hotel.

Follow the by-pass for about 7 km, ignoring the sign to Riyadh at 6 km, until you are under a flyover at a T-junction. Turn left and join the Riyadh road. At this junction there is no sign for Riyadh.

RESET YOUR ODOMETER AT **0**. Drive towards Riyadh. At 32 km on your right are the ruins of an old Turkish fort and then the Arafah garage. Fill up with petrol. At 41.5 km is Exit 54 and the sign to Ashayrah, Mahani and Haden. Exit and turn right. At 43.5 km turn right again and drive to the camel race course about 0.5 km away.

For Ukaz Suq, drive about 1-1.5 km south-west over the sand from the race course and you will see the remains of the doorway arch standing amongst the ruins.

To return to Jeddah via Sayl al Kabir, drive back and rejoin the Taif/Riyadh road at Exit 54. RESET YOUR ODOMETER AT **0**.

At 24 km, turn right to Makkah and Sayl al Kabir. At 28.5 km, turn right again to Makkah, Jeddah and Makir al Sail.

Drive down the gentle gradient through the mountains until, at 85 km, turn right to Jeddah, before the "Muslim only" road to Makkah begins. At approximately 143 km, you pass through Jamoum and straight on for a further 50 or 60 km for Jeddah.

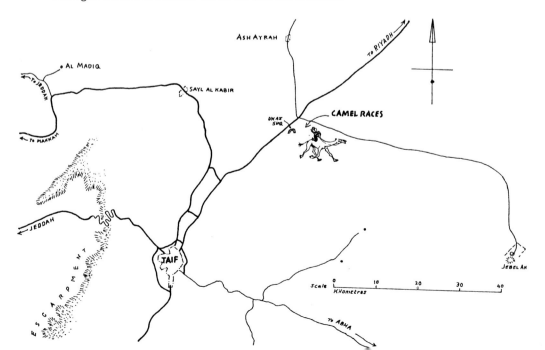

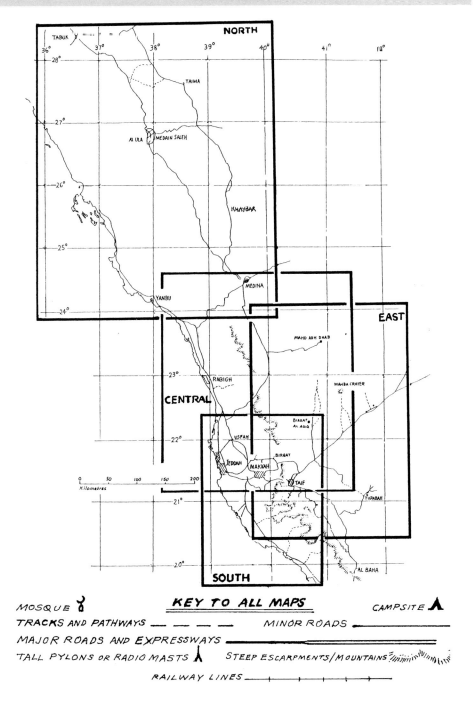

Maps *The Kingdom of Saudi Arabia National Road Atlas and Touring Guide* (Zaki Farsi) is widely available and gives up-to-date coverage of the road system and plenty of geographical and other useful information.

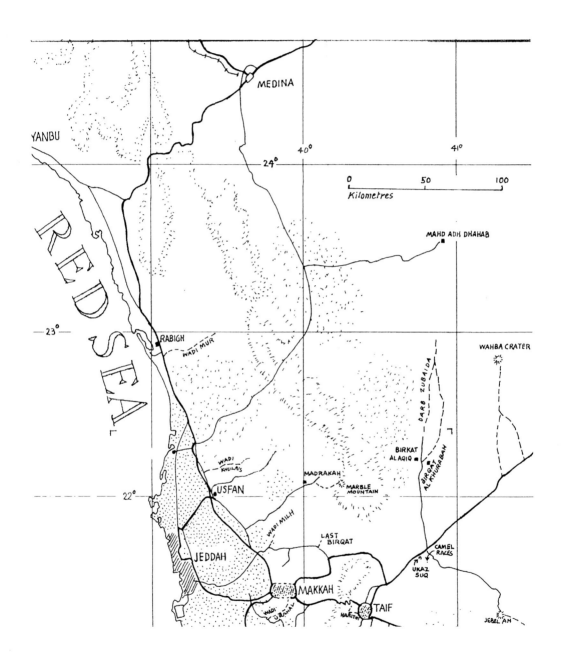

MEDINA

YANBU

40°

41°

24°

0   50   100

Kilometres

MAHD ADH DHAHAB

RED SEA

23°

RABIGH

WADI MUR

WAHBA CRATER

DARB ZUBAIDA

BIRKAT AL AQIQ

BIRQAT AL KHURABAH

WADI KHULAIS

MADRAKAH

MARBLE MOUNTAIN

USFAN

22°

WADI MILH

LAST BIRQAT

CAMEL RACES

JEDDAH

UKAZ SUQ

WADI UBANAH

MAKKAH

HARITH

TAIF

JEBEL AN

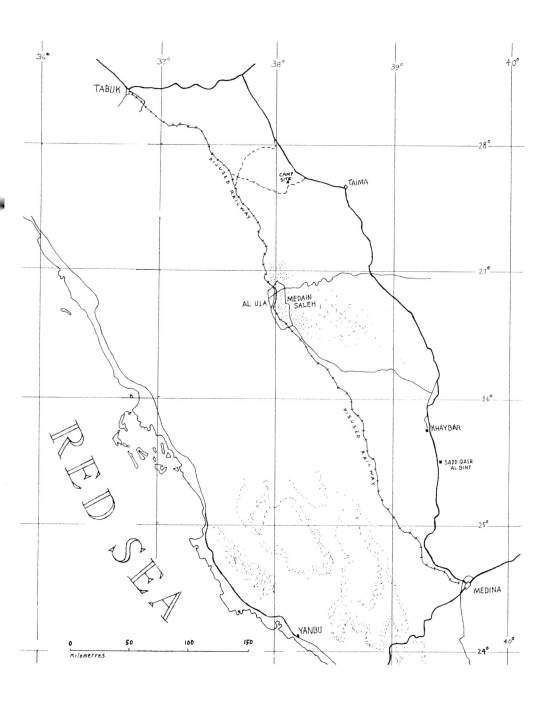

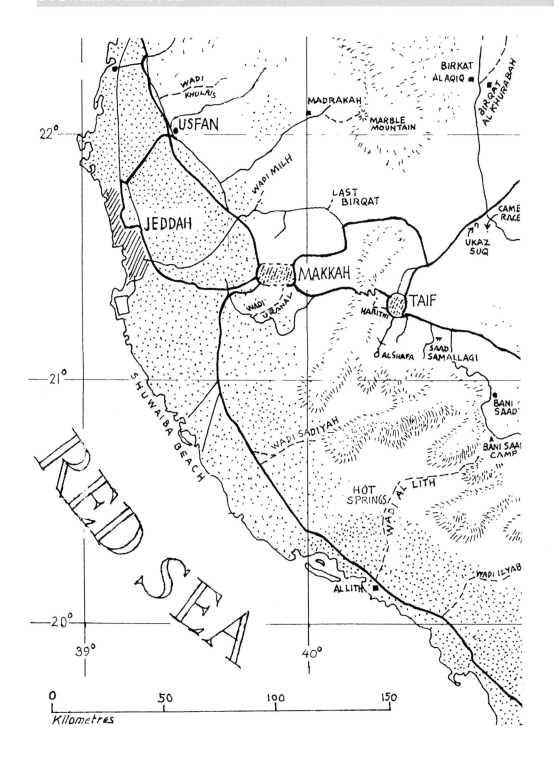

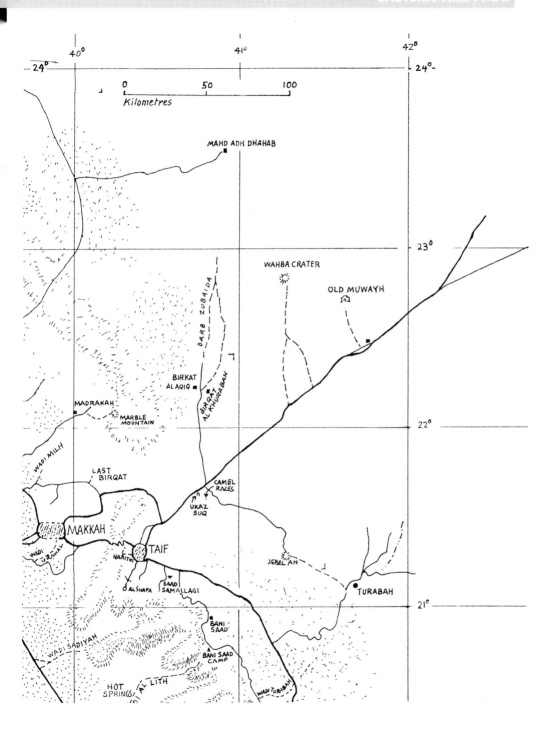

This is a rough guide to trekking and camping from Jeddah. It is written by an enthusiastic novice, not for the already knowledgable, but for those who wish to discover and to experience everything the country has to offer. What is written here has been learned in the three years since 1992, the time when, following the advice and guidance of friends, we first ventured out to sleep under the stars and picnic in some quiet corner of the desert or mountains.

ACKNOWLEDGEMENTS

First I would like to thank Ionis Thompson for encouraging me to embark on the book. Then all those who have contributed to the Jeddah Bushwackers Bulletin over the years, which guided us on many a trip. We owe particular thanks to Nick and Lyn Howarth, who sowed the seeds of our desert infatuation and taught us how to drive in soft sand and over difficult terrain. Also thanks to Nick for providing some of his excellent photographs, and to my son, Sam Barbor, for his sketches featured throughout this book. Our thanks to Robin and Leila Priscott, who have taught us to recognise and record birds seen on some trips; they have opened our eyes to the surprisingly extensive wildlife of Saudi Arabia. I would like to thank all the people who have camped with us, obligingly coming wherever I wanted go - well, almost everywhere. Our most faithful team of campers have been Penny and Ian Brown, (Penny has given us invaluable information on wildlife), Duncan Matthew, who never gives up and cooks an unbeatable pot of porridge, and Alan Barwise with his unflagging enthusiasm. I am most grateful as well to Ulla and Geoff Calvert, who nobly squeezed me into their vehicle and took me to Tabuk, Taima and Medain Saleh, and were regular campers with us before their departure. I would also like to mention the Avison family, whose enchanting little daughters are model campers. Mike lent me cameras and did his best to teach me how to use them. Thanks to Mark Gonzales, I learnt to dive and he generously lent me the gear. Finally, it would have been quite impossible to do this book without my husband, Peter, who has not only had to drive me everywhere, but has advised, checked, suggested and travelled uncomplainingly every weekend he has not been working.

SOURCES

Dr. Saad A. Al-Rashid, *Darb Zubaida, The Pilgrim Road from Kufa to Mecca*, Riyadh University Libraries, 1980.
Bushwackers and Landtrekkers League, Information Bulletin.
M.D. & C.D. Cornes, *The Wild Flowering Plants of Bahrain*, Immel Publishing, 1989.
Department of Antiquities and Museums, *Antiquities of Saudi Arabia*, Ministry of Education, Riyadh 1977.
Charles M. Doughty, *Travels in Arabia Deserta*, Dover Publications Inc. New York, 1979.
Cyril Glasse, *The Concise Encyclopaedia of Islam*, Stacey International, London, 1989.
John Healey, *The Nabataeans and Medain Saleh*, Atlal 10, 1986.
B.J. Hurren, *The Pilgrim Railway into Arabia*, The Railway Magazine, 1965.
Lars Johnsson, *Birds of Europe with North Africa and and Middle East*, Christopher Helm, 1992.
Marycke Jongbloed, *The Living Desert*, Motivate Publishing, 1987.
Joseph Kostiner, *The Making of Saudi Arabia 1916-1936*, Oxford University Press, 1993.
T.E. Lawrence, *Seven Pillars of Wisdom*, Penguin Books, 1962.
Betty Liscombe-Vincett, *Wildflowers of Saudi Arabia*, Immel Publishing, 1977.
Michael McKinnon, *Arabia:Sand, Sea, Sky*, BBC Books, 1990.
Peter Mansfield, *The Arabs*, Penguin Books, 1992.
Elizabeth Monroe, *Philby of Arabia*, Faber, 1973.
Abdallah Adam Nasif, *Al Ula*. King Saud University Press, 1988.
Patrick Pierard, *The Hejaz Waterworks of Ancient Arabia*, Bonjour Jeddah 37, 1995.
Sarah Searight, *Steaming East*, Bodley Head, 1991.

FOR OVER 45 YEARS
WE'VE BEEN MAKING
OUR MARK IN
SAUDI ARABIA

THE SHELL COMPANIES IN SAUDI ARABIA

The archaeological wonder of Medain Saleh

The weekend – or longer – expeditions in this handbook were collated from notes made by the author and others over several years travelling out of Jeddah up to 1995, when all information was verified as up-to-date.

The rich rewards of local knowledge and points of interest in Saudi Arabia's history, archaeology, landscape, and geology are here made attainable by all who live in Jeddah with the time and energy to set forth and discover.

This book has been published as a sister volume to "Desert Treks from Riyadh" by Ionis Thompson, also published by
STACEY INTERNATIONAL

Patricia Barbor

STACEY INTERNATIONAL
LONDON

ISBN 0-905743-89-X

9 780905 743899 >